The Business Rule Revolution

Running Business the Right Way

Editors:
Barbara von Halle
Larry Goldberg

Guest Contribution:
John Zachman

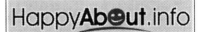

21265 Stevens Creek Blvd.
Suite 205
Cupertino, CA 95014

The Business Rule Revolution

First Printing: October 2006
ISBN 1-60005-013-1
Place of Publication: Silicon Valley, California, USA
Library of Congress Number: 2001012345

Trademarks

Warning and Disclaimer

Publisher

- Mitchell Levy, http://www.happyabout.info/

Executive Editors

- Barbara von Halle, http://www.kpiusa.com/
- Larry Goldberg, http://www.kpiusa.com/

Copy Edititor

- Jennifer Finger, http://www.keenreader.com/

Cover Designer

- Cate Calson, http://www.calsongraphics.com/

Layout Designer

- Val Swisher, President, Oak Hill Corporation
  http://www.oakhillcorporation.com/

A Message From Happy About®

Thank you for your purchase of this Happy About book. It is available online at http://HappyAbout.info/business-rule-revolution.php or at other online and physical bookstores.

- Please contact us for quantity discounts at sales@happyabout.info
- If you want to be informed by e-mail of upcoming Happy About® books, please e-mail bookupdate@happyabout.info
- If you want to contribute to upcoming Happy About® books, please go to http://happyabout.info/contribute/

Happy About is interested in you if you are an author who would like to submit a non-fiction book proposal or a corporation that would like to have a book written for you. Please contact us by e-mail editorial@happyabout.info or phone (1-408-257-3000).

Other Happy About books available include:

- Happy About Global Software Test Automation: http://www.happyabout.info/globalswtestautomation.php
- Happy About Joint Venturing: http://happyabout.info/jointventuring.php
- Happy About LinkedIn for Recruiting: http://happyabout.info/linkedin4recruiting.php
- Happy About Website Payments with PayPal http://happyabout.info/paypal.php
- Happy About Outsourcing http://happyabout.info/outsourcing.php
- Happy About Knowing What to Expect in 2006 http://happyabout.info/economy.php

Other soon-to-be-released Happy About books include:

- Happy About CEO Excellence: http://happyabout.info/ceo-excellence.php
- Happy About Working After 60: http://happyabout.info/working-after-60.php
- Happy About Open Source: http://happyabout.info/opensource.php

Acknowledgments

No book is possible without the support of personal and professional comrades. This book is no exception.

From a historical perspective, we wish to acknowledge those who defined and pursued the fields of knowledge engineering and artificial intelligence, paving the way to understanding intelligence, such as Patrick Winston. Also, from a historical perspective, this book owes acknowledgement to the pioneering vendors of business rule engine technology, some of which no longer exist while others are in found in these pages.

Of great significance to this book are the contributors, of course, who gave of their time and experience, meeting various deadlines most graciously. Deserving of special mention is John Zachman, who found time in his incredibly demanding schedule, to provide us with a valuable chapter on Enterprise Architecture.

We also wish to thank those who financially sponsored the book, up front and unseen: ILOG, Inc., Fair Isaac Corporation, and InScope Solutions Inc.

We could not have brought this book from vision to reality without the patience and creativity of Mitchell Levy and excellent work by Jennifer Finger, Cate Calson, and Christine Milbank.

Our greatest acknowledgement belongs to you, the readers. It is your interest and your vision in the Business Rules Approach that gave birth to this book and will keep it going.

Dedication

This book is dedicated to our spouses, Mike and Jill, for their enduring patience.

c o n t e n t s

Part III The Technology Side of Business Rules

Part IV | **Wrap Up**

An Important Letter from the Editors: Is the Business Rule Revolution Real?

Barbara von Halle and Larry Goldberg

What Did We Learn From This Book?

Without a doubt, every contributor to this book is a hero in their own right. Each has a story to tell. Each has been responsible for business rule successes. Each has witnessed business rule mistakes. None are afraid to share both good and bad so that readers can grow from their experiences.

Together, common lessons emerge:

- Business rules are an under-valued asset at most organizations today.

- Business rules may hold the key to organizational agility, consistency, and organizational knowledge, if not organizational intelligence and integrity.

- Business rules are related to, but separate from, process and information (or data).

- The "decision" emerges as the missing link in methodologies by which business rules become visible and manageable.

- The Business Rules Approach has many versions in practice, requires new skills, and aims to bring IT and the business closer together.

But, Is There Truly a Business Rule Revolution Taking Place?

Commonality alone does not a revolution make. Rather, we see evidence of a revolution in a most unlikely place: the intriguing discrepancies and their impact on businesses.

The major discrepancy, surfacing across chapters in this book, is the answer to the **one** key question: W*ho ought to be the operational managers and authors of business rules as those rules are to operate in the business and in its systems?*

On one hand, the answer is a **rule analyst** who is an intermediary. Such a rule analyst translates business words from other business sources into a business rule construct that can be acted upon by a human, but mostly by a system. This rule author has a business background and a level of technical background, but is not as technically-oriented as a programmer or object modeler.

On the other hand, the answer is a **business policy maker** who serves both as the business source of business words and as translator, without the intervention of a rule analyst. This rule author is a business operations person with a strong business background, such as an underwriter, legal representative, or product manager.

This distinction makes all the difference in the world regarding the ultimate impact of the Business Rules Approach and technology on a business. It will differentiate market leaders from followers and losers. It will handle more easily Zachman's escalating complexity and change (see Chapter 3).

The second answer requires business policy makers to see the power of their enhanced role and have the willingness to accept responsibility for it. The second answer also requires technical experts to encourage that desire, welcome that new business role, and deliver and support the technical infrastructure to make it happen.

This is precisely where the storm is brewing (see Chapter 15). There remains conflict in this area in most places, although not in all places. This is precisely why we believe we are at the brink of a Business Rule Revolution, and why the Rule Maturity Model (RMM) focuses on this line in the sand—the line between business policy makers and business rule translators that is disappearing.

Planning an Organization's Part in the Business Rule Revolution

Two of the RMM's vectors originate from the business (i.e., business control and business value of business rules). The third vector of the RMM (i.e., the technical state of business rules) at any level enables the business control and business value of the rules at that level.

While the RMM, by itself is not a report card, business competition will occur over RMM levels. That is, as one organization matures along the RMM, that organization raises the bar for its competition. Therefore, over time it will become more important to achieve higher levels of the RMM. This is more likely to be successful when an organization passes through lower levels along the way. That is why, today, both answers to the **one** key question are correct – because organizations are taking the journey one step at a time. Some organizations are further along in that journey. That is why, in the future, the second answer will be more correct.

One More Time: Is the Business Rule Revolution Real?

According to the Encarta Dictionary (English, North America), there are four definitions for revolution.

The first is "overthrow of government: overthrow of a ruler or political system." In a business rule world, the word "ruler" couldn't be more appropriate. In a business rule world, this definition implies a more direct, powerful, and balanced political system, defined by rules, and driven more by business people and goals than by technology experts and technology constraints.

The second definition of revolution is "major change: a dramatic change in ideas and practices." Notice that this definition is about new ideas and corresponding practices. New practices around business rule management are emerging and the enterprise perspective is becoming intriguing.

The third definition for revolution is "a circle around something: a complete circle made around something, such as the orbit made by a planet or satellite around another body." We are, in fact, circling back around the business rules in the center. Before there were computers, business leaders set policies and rules, often based on trial-and-error until the rules seemed to work sufficiently. Along came information technology, and with all good intentions, we automated those policies and rules without their changing much. We buried them in technology where many became lost and unknown. The Business Rule Revolution circles back, giving those policies and rules back to the rightful parties so those parties can rule more effectively in today's world, where these policies and rules need to change often and on demand.

The final definition of revolution is a "period of major geological change: a period during which the Earth's crust changes considerably and major features such as mountain ranges may emerge." This definition, perhaps, says it all.

Where Can We Find It?

No matter how you look at it, the Business Rule Revolution is happening. If you look closely, it is changing the crust of the business world as we know it. New, business-empowered products and features are emerging as organizations embark on their business rule journey.

Look for them in the pages of this book!

Contributing Authors

Contributors of this edition of the Business Rule Revolution, in alphabetical order, are:

May Abraham is the founder of a management consulting firm, Global Knowledge Architects, focused on helping companies manage and implement their core business knowledge using a Business Rules Approach and structured methodologies. May is a senior Knowledge manager and has more than fifteen years of experience in the knowledge management areas including business rules, geographic information systems, business analytics and decision support systems. In her former job at AIG as Director, knowledge management, she guided many strategic business rules projects and has successfully established enterprise wide methodologies and implementations. May has a Masters degree in Mathematics from Annamalai University, India.

Michael Beck is President of Organization Solutions Inc., and a business executive and senior management consultant with over twenty-five years' experience in both consulting and line management in commercial and government positions. His broad experience includes strategic planning, business reengineering; requirements development and management, business rules methodology, and management process development. Michael has applied his knowledge and experience to the modernization of tax administration systems in both federal and state governments.

Larry Goldberg is Managing Partner of Knowledge Partners, Inc., specializing in business strategy and architecture. Larry has over thirty years of experience in entrepreneurship on three continents—Africa, Europe and North America. In the last twenty three years his focus has been in creating rules-based technologies and applications. He has sponsored and played a primary architectural role in Business Rules Management Systems, and business rules-based commercial software applications in healthcare, supply chain, property and casualty insurance, and taxation regulation. Prior to joining Knowledge Partners, Inc. in 2005 as Managing Partner, he sold his company, PowerFlex Software, to Sapiens Americas, Inc., in 1999, becoming a Senior Vice President of Sapiens.

Barbara von Halle is the Founder and Managing Partner of Knowledge Partners Inc. As a recognized leader in today's Business Rules Approach, Barbara led the development of the best-selling Business Rules methodology book (*Business Rules Applied*, 2002: John Wiley & Sons), the KPI STEP™ licensed product of Business Rules Management methods and tools, the KPI RMM™, and a proven approach for excavating rules from code. As a Business Rules pioneer, Barbara received the Outstanding Individual Achievement Award from the International Data Management Association. She has earned a bachelor's degree in mathematics and an master's degree in computer science with an electrical engineering focus.

Neal McWhorter is a Principal at Enterprise Agility. Neal helps organizations transform their business goals into business solutions. He has worked with numerous large organizations to help them realize their goals of achieving greater business agility by helping them adopt a business engineering approach. The Enterprise Agility Business Engineering approach allows an organization's business process and rules to bridge the business/IT divide and become the actual implementation on which the business operates.

Jordan Masanga is IT Quality Assurance Manager and Technology Officer of Oregon Public Employees Retirement System (OPERS). Jordan has directed OPERS in implementing QA best practices, IBM Rational Unified Process® (RUP®), business process management initiatives, and automated workflow for over three years. He has over eighteen years' experience in information and high technology, specifically software development and systems integration. He was previously a Vice President and Director of Engineering, Quality and Process of ADC Telecommunications, where he managed a division with five distributed international offices.

Art Moore is a Managing Partner of Clear Systems LLC. Art has over twenty years of IT experience, from systems development to IT strategic planning and practice management. He has focused extensively on assisting large projects and organizations to establish and integrate business rule-related system specification and development methods, technology, and management tools and processes in their total business systems development and management context. Mr. Moore is a co-author of Barbara von Halle's last book, *Business Rules Applied* (2002: John Wiley & Sons).

Linda Nieporent is BRMS Product Manager at ILOG, Inc. Linda has over ten years of IT experience, the last six focused on business rules, both from a business user perspective and an IT implementation perspective. Ms. Nieporent is a co-author of Barbara von Halle's last book, *Business Rules Applied* (2002: John Wiley & Sons). As an active proponent of business rules practices, she has written articles and presented on business rules-related topics at user groups and industry conferences.

John Semmel is Designer and Developer of Rating and Quoting Applications at Aetna. John has spent more than twenty-eight years in IT, the last ten at Aetna where he spent four years working with business rules. He also spent several years at EDS on a team that developed a mainframe-based, rules-driven rating and underwriting application in the late 1980's to early 1990's.

Brian Stucky is Vice President of Business Rule Solutions at InScope Solutions, Inc. Brian has nearly two decades of experience designing and implementing business rule systems and directs the company's business rule practice area. Prior to joining InScope Solutions, Brian served as the Enterprise Rule Steward at Freddie Mac where he set the business and technology strategy for business rule development across the corporation. Brian also co-founded two companies that specialized in the design and implementation of intelligent systems.

James Taylor is Vice President of Enterprise Decision Management (EDM) at Fair Isaac Corporation. James is widely recognized as a leading proponent of the Enterprise Decision Management approach that uses business rules and predictive analytics to deliver excellence in operational decision making. James has experience in all aspects of software development. He previously worked at a start-up, in PeopleSoft's R&D group and at Ernst and Young. He writes and speaks extensively on EDM and is often quoted and interviewed.

Gene Weng is Business Rule Lead in a major American financial service company. Gene also worked as an IT architect for Perot Systems. He holds a master's degree in mathematics from the University of Science and Technology, Beijing, and a master's degree in computer science from the University of Oregon.

Larry Ward is Quality Assurance Project Manager at Oregon Public Employees Retirement Systems. Larry has over forty years' experience in systems analysis and design, industrial engineering, and QA, including over ten years' Business Rules Approach experience. He is working on a major systems conversion project that implements BPM at OPERS and uses the OPERS Business Rules Approach. Larry designed the process to apply a Business Rules Approach at OPERS and was the project coordinator for five years; he managed IBM® Rational® RequisitePro® and ClearCase® database repositories, requirements, and content for over five years, and assisted in developing tools and processes to update the rule databases. He has earned a bachelor's degree in business and management, a master's degree in management, and a Juris Doctor degree.

John A. Zachman is CEO of Zachman Institute for Framework Advancement, Chairman of the Board of Zachman Framework Associates, and operator of Zachman International. John is well-known as the originator of the "Framework for Enterprise Architecture" which has received broad acceptance around the world as an integrative framework, or "periodic table," of descriptive representations for Enterprises. He is also known for his early contributions to IBM's Information Strategy methodology (Business Systems Planning) as well as to their executive team planning techniques (Intensive Planning). John serves on the Executive Council for Information Management and Technology of the United States General Accounting Office. He is a Fellow for the College of Business Administration of the University of North Texas; he serves on the Advisory Board for the Data Resource Management Program at the University of Washington and on the Advisory Board of the Data Administration Management Association International (DAMA-I), from whom he won the 2002 Lifetime Achievement Award. He was awarded the 2004 Oakland University Applied Technology in Business (ATIB) Award for IS Excellence and Innovation. He is the author of the e-Book *The Zachman Framework for Enterprise Architecture: A Primer on Enterprise Engineering and Manufacturing.*

Introduction: Welcome to the Business Rule Revolution

Barbara von Halle

Why This Book?

Business rules are everywhere. The right ones bring success, represent the smartest thinking, and make people such as customers feel good. The wrong rules bring trouble and uncertainty. You never know when the wrong rules may strike. You probably don't even know which ones they are.

Obviously, business rules are the very core of any business and determine whether it succeeds and how well, or fails and how badly. And yet, the current state of business rule best practices in the marketplace is unknown, until this book. This book is part of a series destined to be the Voice of the Business Rule Revolution, sharing and measuring its progress.

The Business Rule Revolution is the awakening of business leaders to the importance of business integrity and governance through management of individual rules. Some organizations are making great investments in it. Some have not begun. And most, are somewhere in the middle. But, there is no published book to serve as an anchor point—a book where real people share real experiences so that the Business Rule Revolution does its job.

Six important aspects of the book are:

1. It is for managers and decision-makers who make things happen in their organizations.

2. It addresses business rules to be leveraged for agility, compliance, and corporate intelligence as a key mechanism for engineering the business itself.

3. It is not meant to be read cover-to-cover.

4. Together, the sections provide a step-by-step management approach that crosses business and information technology barriers.

5. Real case studies are written by real people as practiced in well-respected corporations, government agencies, consultancies, and software vendors.

6. Leading technology is highlighted.

Who Is This Book For?

This book is for anyone interested in starting, planning, learning about, or participating in the Business Rule Revolution. These are the people who see the value and want to be part of it.

How Is This Book Unique?

There is no book like this one in the business rule space. Its uniqueness is that no one person wrote it. It is a true anthology of experiences, successes and of disappointments, but full of practical guidance, contributed by everyday people.

Goals of This Book

As the first book in the series, the goals of this book are to:

- Expose the practicality of the Business Rules Approach through successes in major organizations

- Bring business and information technology professionals together

- Present the achievements from a Business Rules Approach for both business and information technology

Who Wrote This Book?

Most of the people who wrote this book are not professional writers, teachers or speakers, although some of them present at Business Rules- and related conferences. They are not theorists, although some have formal education in fields related to business rules, such as artificial intelligence, knowledge engineering, and software engineering. Most of them don't know each other. The one common characteristic they share is their generosity in disclosing their business rule lives to you.

While only a few chapters have been coordinated with other chapters, together they tell a true and complete story. The story has a business side and a technical side. These sides come together in these pages, to be shared by business and technical people. Our hope is that it brings these people together to realize the same business goals through business rules.

How to Read This Book

The book has three sections.

For both *business and technical audiences*, Section 1 is an introduction to business rule topics. As such, it summarizes the current and desired state of practitioners of the Business Rules Approach. It explains the Rule Maturity Model (KPI RMM™), where the marketplace is on that model today, and where it wants to go. The Rule Maturity Model is a prevalent theme throughout many of the chapters.

Section 1 also contains a pivotal chapter from John Zachman, clarifying the concept of Enterprise Architecture which is the application of traditional architecture principles to an enterprise, not merely technology. From here, Larry Goldberg's chapter presents the role of business rules in an organization's Enterprise Architecture.

For the **business audience**, Section 2 focuses on understanding business processes and insights into the business policy maker as rule author. Specifically, Neal McWhorter explains business engineering with business rules, Art Moore and Michael Beck uncover the integration of business process modeling and business rules, and Larry Ward and Jordan Masanga explain how business process management (BPM) activities improve the business (with ties to business rules). A very special chapter from John Semmel describes home-grown software, by which non-technical rule authors conceive, author, analyze, and simulate rules.

For the more **technical audience**, Section 3 covers topics about rule architecture and technical rule support. Starting off, Gene Weng and May Abraham each contribute a chapter on the role and importance of the rule architect and rule architecture when building complex rule systems. Brian Stucky, representing a business rules service company called InScope Solutions, provides insights into positioning an enterprise for business rules in terms of people, processes, and organization. It is in Section 3 that software vendors present technology solutions to business rule opportunities. Two leading business rule management system (BRMS) vendors are highlighted in this section. James Taylor, representing Fair Isaac Corporation, describes the use of business rule technology in delivering an enterprise policy hub. Linda Nieporent, representing ILOG, presents a case study with Equifax as it evolved in its use of ILOG's BRMS. Both vendors and their products have been around and evolved for several decades. They have much experience to share and interesting strategic visions for the Business Rule Revolution. Also in this section is a description of the KPI STEP™ Workbench as a source rule repository supporting organizations at Level 2 of the Rule Maturity Model.

The Open Door | Hopefully, this book is the first in a long series. We welcome new contributors and chapters. The journey begins today. Make this book, these authors, and this series your business rule almanac.

Sincerely,

Barbara von Halle
Larry Goldberg

Part I
The Compelling World of Business Rules

Appropriate for both business and technical audiences, this section is an introduction to business rule topics. Its four chapters cover an explanation of the KPI Rule Maturity Model™ (Chapter 1), the current and target states of current practices based on a survey (Chapter 2), Enterprise architecture as a non-technical business-critical discipline (Chapter 3), and the role of business rules in such architecture (Chapter 4).

In their own words, below are quotes selected by each author to provide the reader with insights into each chapter:

"The Business Rules Approach makes possible the opportunity to manage the most important rules of the business, no matter what kind they are or what kind of technology they best belong in, if any.....The KPI Rule Maturity Model™ is a tested roadmap by which organizations set realistic business rule expectations and design a practical roadmap for getting there.... Through the RMM, the vision of the Business Rules Approach will be realized: *To enable business leadership to take control of the guiding levers of the enterprise, and enable technology to match the rate of business change.*"

Chapter 1, Barbara von Halle

"The most common target state for [RMM survey] participants is RMM Level 2. Higher levels of the RMM are achievable, but rare today. Achieving RMM Level 3 usually requires home-grown software. Therefore, more software advances are needed and expected for enabling rule management and authoring by the business's true business rule stewards."

Chapter 2, Barbara von Halle

"I don't think there is any question about whether an enterprise is going to do enterprise architecture or not; that is, it will not be optional if an enterprise intends to be viable in the Information Age. The only question is when they will start working on enterprise architecture, because there potentially is a lot of work to do-and at the point in time the enterprise is going to need it, it is going to be too late to do it! Business rules may well be a good place to start working on it."

Chapter 3, John Zachman

"The architecture should reflect the need to place the business firmly in control of business rules, and the greater the maturity that the enterprise needs to achieve, the greater the role of the business in managing the rules."

Chapter 4, Larry Goldberg

1 The Essential Business Rule Roadmap

Barbara von Halle

What is the Business Rule Revolution?

The Business Rule Revolution is happening everywhere, even if it seems invisible. In fact, the business rules that are unseen or unknown are precisely the ones that can do the most damage. Invisible rules lurk behind a lack of proper business rule management—creating a precarious business climate for these times.

Consider the growing and painful awareness of questionable accounting practices by some corporate executives in some major organizations. What is at play here? Business rules are at play—good or bad, known or unknown. In these cases, rules were broken or secret. Some were improper rules applied to achieve improper objectives. Think of the Business Rule Revolution as appropriate parties knowing what the rules are, applying the rules in all the right places, and the organization therefore taking full responsibility for its rules and its integrity.

In a nutshell, the Business Rule Revolution represents an emerging undeniable need for the right people to know what a business's rules are, to be able to change those rules on demand according to changing objectives, to be accountable for those rules, and to predict as closely as possible the impact of rule changes on the business, its customers, its partners, its competition, and its regulators.

This means that the Business Rule Revolution reflects a pent-up need for business people to play a more prominent role in safely stewarding the business's rules from their inception to execution, with probable automation. Otherwise, the business is driving in the dark, off-road without headlights—an environment where serious accidents can happen. An organization aiming to better manage its important business rules needs a goal, a roadmap, and a plan for action. This is where KPI's Rule Maturity Model (KPI RMM™ or RMM) fits.

This chapter explains the KPI Rule Maturity Model as the essential roadmap by which organizations chart their course in the Business Rule Revolution. This chapter covers:

- What exactly are business rules?

- What is the Business Rules Approach?

- Putting the business first

- What is the Rule Maturity Model?

- What the Rule Maturity Model is not

- How the Rule Maturity Model is used today

- Today's leaders: RMM levels 1, 2

- Tomorrow's leaders: RMM levels 3, 4, 5

- The Rule Maturity Model and the changing relationship between business and IT

- What happens next-technology predictions in the Rule Maturity Model

- Summary and future vision

What Exactly Are Business Rules?

Business Rules are the ultimate levers with which business management is able to guide and control the business. In fact, the business's rules are the means by which an organization implements competitive strategy, promotes policy, and complies with legal obligations.

In reality, not every business rule is worth explicitly stating or even automating. Also, while business rule management systems (BRMS) are extremely valuable, not all business rules belong in one. A critical aspect of a successful Business Rules Approach, therefore, is assessing the value of specific business rules to the business, how often those rules need to change, how urgently the change is needed, and how much control the business people need or want over those changes, from start to finish.

The following are examples of business rules or business policies as a business person might initially express them:

- A premium customer is every customer whose credit rating is A or B.

- If a premium customer requests a loan for greater than $500,000, allow a delay in the first payment date by 30 days.

- The formula for computing a student's cumulative grade-point average is found on page 6 of the student policy manual.

- A driver should proceed in a particular direction if the street is labeled "senso unico," but can proceed in the opposite direction without penalty unless the driver causes an accident.

- If a loan applicant's outside credit rating is marginal and the applicant also has a credit card balance greater than $5,000, then it is highly likely that the applicant will default on a loan.

- An employee who has completed five years of full-time employment with the company is entitled to four weeks of paid vacation.

- Stock options vest at a rate of one-third each year over three years.

- A customer with outstanding payments due must pay in full prior to a new order being shipped.

- A preferred customer automatically receives free express shipping on all orders.

These examples illustrate that there are different kinds of business rules. Some rules impose constraints (constraint rules), some provide suggestions (guideline rules), some make calculations (computation rules), some infer interim conclusions (inferred knowledge rules), and some infer actions (action-enabler rules).

What is the Business Rules Approach?

There have been generations of advances in business and software engineering techniques and technology; yet, the rules of most businesses remain lost, unknown, inconsistent, inadequate, or simply resistant to change. Such rules, if crucial to business operations, are a hidden liability. Unmanaged rules result in lost time-to-market, regulation violations, and customer dissatisfaction: a sub-optimal running of the business at best.

Today, the Business Rules Approach is best defined as a formal way of managing and automating an organization's business rules so that the business behaves and evolves as its leaders intend. Organizations today apply the Business Rules Approach to rules carried out by humans during the course of manual processes as well as those automated in systems. Therefore, the Business Rules Approach enables business leaders to confirm that the right rules are guiding the business in all of the right places. This becomes possible by identifying rule-rich business processes and understanding the importance of the rules that are to guide specific aspects of those processes.

The Business Rules Approach includes tasks, roles, and a rule repository for business people, rules engines for automation, and formal ways of expressing rules so that the business's policies and supporting rules can be quantified, accessed, and changed as needed.

When the Business Rules Approach results in the automation of rules in systems, often a business rule management system (BRMS) is deployed. Applying the Business Rules Approach with a BRMS "builds better, changeable systems faster than any previous approach."[1] Real-world experience proves not only that business rule projects are completed faster, at less cost, and with less risk, but they continue to deliver substantial savings in time and money because rule maintenance is significantly accelerated.

Putting the Business First

While the Business Rules Approach has wide applicability, it always begins with the business itself, specifically its goals. After all, business rules existed long before there were computers. The Business Rules Approach recognizes that business rules are first about business directions, and later about databases and engines. With this perspective in mind, the Business Rules Approach makes possible the opportunity to manage the most important rules of the business, no matter what kind they are or what kind of technology they best belong in, if any.

---

1. von Halle, Barbara, <u>Business Rules Applied</u> (2002: John Wiley & Sons, New York)

This means that the adoption of the Business Rules Approach starts by understanding business objectives and letting those objectives drive the business rule management practices that are optimum for the organization or project.

To be business-centric, the Business Rules Approach requires a source rule repository. A source rule repository provides the following:

- Storage of rules for the business audience, in a central or coordinated location

- Access to rules by anyone who needs to know them

- Analysis of rule sets for redundancy, inconsistency, etc.

- Involvement of all stakeholders in the rule change process

- Traceability to where rules are executing in the business and its systems

- Traceability of business rules to relevant items, such as processes, use cases, decisions, business terms, data fields, stakeholders, motivations, data, and object models.

Critical to the Business Rules Approach is a newly defined business rule life cycle. It starts with a business opportunity or challenge, moves through the articulation of policies and rules with a business focus, and may culminate in automated rules in systems. The newly defined business rule life cycle typically enables shorter change cycles and may shift more of the responsibility for stewarding rule changes from technical to business people.

The optimum business rule management practices will enable management of underlying business rules by appropriate business stewards, regardless of what kinds of rules they turn out to be, what kind of rule authoring techniques will work best, and what kinds of technology options might be optimal. The optimum business rule management practices should therefore be designed to fit an organization's or project's goals and culture. This brings us to the role of the RMM.

What is the Rule Maturity Model?

Essentially, the RMM is a simple and practical model by which an organization aligns its business objectives with the optimum business rule management practices for achieving those objectives. It provides a straight-forward roadmap, customizable for each organization or project.

Like other maturity models, the RMM has six levels, starting from 0 and leading to 5. In a level 0 organization, people are unaware that business rules have a value worth contemplating; at level 5, organizations are utilizing business rules as proactive and predictive levers for change and compliance, as well as for gaining momentum over the competition, and predicting the future. Therefore, each RMM level represents an alignment between specific organizational objectives and corresponding business rule management practices, supported by refined roles, techniques, and software requirements. Each level also represents a major change in an organization's culture and its ability to reach for higher goals. Therefore, skipping levels is not recommended.

At a glance, each level of the RMM represents one major goal with respect to business rule management, as depicted in Figure 1 and listed below:

- RMM Level 1 ➔ Knowledge of Rules
- RMM Level 2 ➔ Agility of Rules
- RMM Level 3 ➔ Consistency and Alignment of Rules
- RMM Level 4 ➔ Prediction of Rules
- RMM Level 5 ➔ Stewardship of Rules.

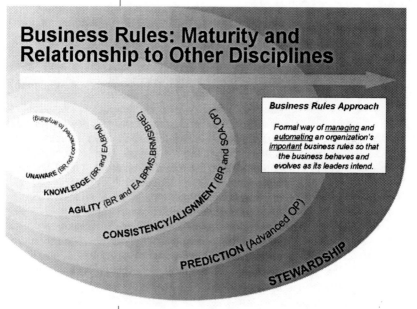

Figure 1: The RMM at a Glance

What the Rule Maturity Model is Not

The RMM is not a report card. In fact, higher RMM levels are not necessarily better than lower ones. It would be incorrect to judge organizations or projects seeking or achieving lower levels of the RMM as falling short in any way. To the contrary, applying the RMM successfully means achieving the RMM level that delivers desired business objectives through the managing of related business rules.

Figure 2 depicts more details of the RMM[2], along three vectors. The first vector is the business value which addresses the influence over rule changes materialized by each RMM level. The second vector is the technical state which describes where rules reside and how they are managed at each level. The third vector is the business control which alludes to the role of non-technical rule stewards and how that role evolves at each level of the RMM.

---

2. The original version of the RMM is at www.kpiusa.com/rmm.htm

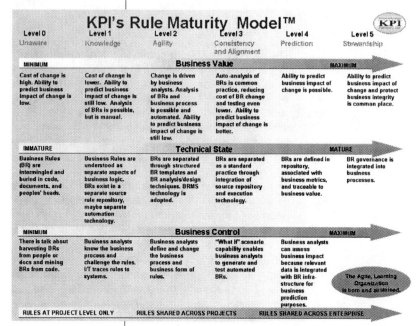

Figure 2: The RMM in More Detail

How the Rule Maturity Model is Used Today

To date, various organizations use the RMM for one or more of four main purposes:

- <u>Assess their current state</u> to understand where they are today with respect to managing business rules. Most are at RMM Level 0.

- <u>Define their target state</u> to determine how far they should go in managing business rules. Most are aiming for RMM Level 1 or 2, with a few aiming for RMM Level 3.

- <u>Certify achievement</u> to publicize to internal and external audiences their successes as they achieve targeted RMM levels.

Chapter 1: The Essential Business Rule Roadmap

- <u>Determine the business value of incorporating the Business Rules Approach</u> to drive the adoption of the Business Rules Approach by targeted business objectives and to determine the means and metrics of measuring its outcome.

Organizations using the RMM to assess current and target states begin by identifying business objectives to be achieved by managing business rules. This leads to answers to the following questions before determining the desired target RMM Level:

- What objectives are achievable by better managing business rules?

- What are the short-term and long-term timeframes for achieving those objectives?

- Which business rules are worth managing?

- Who is to play which roles in managing business rules? Specifically, who drives policies to new and changed rules for different parts of the business?

- Is there a need for joint stewardship for some policies and rules?

- How will political conflicts concerning rules be settled?

- What technology is needed to support each of the roles?

Use of the RMM to certify achievement of specific RMM levels has uncovered a critical consideration. The RMM implies that all three vectors be managed at the same level of maturity. That is, there is danger in achioving an RMM Level 3 for the technical state (I.e., delivering enterprise-worthy rule authoring software, etc.) but an RMM Level 2 for the business control vector (i.e., putting that technology into the wrong hands). Inconsistent maturity causes unexpected, possibly devastating havoc. An organization exhibiting disparate RMM levels in its business rule management may be dysfunctional, putting anticipated benefits in jeopardy. In fact, most

advantage of BRMS deployment because rules are expressed in a more rigorous form, closer to that needed for automation and for automated rule analysis (available through BRMS). To achieve maximum agility, a Level 2 organization requires traceability from changing rules to other business and system artifacts. Thus, Level 2 requires separation and traceability of business rules to support business and technical agility.

Organizations aiming for Level 2 store these rules in a more sophisticated source rule repository, used by business and technical people. The source rule repository also captures standard terms and related reusable rule clauses, enabling more robust rule reporting and analysis. Rule related roles are defined. Project-level rule stewardship exists. Typically, a BRMS is used for some automated rules.

The transition to Level 2 involves adding the authoring, validating, and analyzing of rules with an underlying semantic model. In some Level 2 organizations, business analysts who are not so technically oriented may author the business-friendly form of a rule, especially if the source rule repository is one that is easy to use. Still, technically-oriented business analysts usually write the more formal form while technical people convert these into an automated form. The responsibility for creating business rules is shared by business analysts and technical people.

Tomorrow's Leaders: RMM Levels 3, 4, 5

**Level 3:
Consistency
and Alignment**

An organization aiming for RMM Level 3 seeks *consistency* among its rules and *alignment* of them to current and changing objectives. Therefore, an RMM Level 3 organization seeks business rule governance across projects, systems, and perhaps business unit boundaries.

Such an organization identifies business-driven benefits for standardizing or sharing business rule techniques and even automated business rule services across projects. These organizations typically establish a Business Rules Center of Excellence that endorses a standard business rules methodology. Sometimes multiple BRMSs are deployed, and common business rules techniques, standards, and roles are shared across BRMSs, when appropriate.

The transition to RMM Level 3 is extremely significant as it means cross-organizational rule governance as well as more sophisticated source rule repository support. It implies organizational change and collaboration, and brings with it some of the greatest business rule benefits.

Level 3 introduces automated rule analysis and simulation capabilities. This means that the translation from the business-friendly form to an executable version is either prompted by intelligent software or automatic in some manner. In this environment, business analysts or even business experts are able to author, change, and test rules without relying on technical people to bridge the gap. Usually, technical people put the resulting rules in production.

| **Level 4:** | An organization at RMM Level 4 sees business rules |
| **Predictions** | as *predictions* for future success. Business people or |

Level 4:
Predictions

An organization at RMM Level 4 sees business rules as *predictions* for future success. Business people or analysts hypothesize about future events to which they wish to respond in a carefully pre-calculated manner. Business leaders or analysts craft different rule sets, test, simulate and compare predictions, and have these rule sets ready-and-waiting for deployment in anticipation of related threats and opportunities. These people craft business rules to react to such events and predict the business impact of rule changes on the client base, revenue, profit, and staff levels.

Level 4 opens up a whole new world. A Level 4 organization supports a variety of tools for capturing and analyzing rules and with metrics against which desired impact of rules on the business are managed. Business analysts or business experts define their destination via metrics and then interactively craft the rules by which they hope to arrive there. With tools and metrics at hand, business analysts or business experts can now proceed confidently from understanding future business objectives to simulating rules within a future context. Again, usually technical people put such rules into production, when needed.

Level 5:
Stewardship

An organization aiming at RMM Level 5 embraces the full *stewardship* of business rules for refining and re-inventing itself as necessary. The difference between Level 4 and 5 is that Level 4 aims at immediate or short-term futures, whereas Level 5 looks to a variety of longer-term futures. It represents a world of anticipation and planned reaction while hitting the ultimate goal of agility. A Level 5 organization is not satisfied in just being fast, but plans on being first. A Level 5 organization defines various futures as the organizations wishes them to play out before they happen!

The characteristics of each level of the RMM are summarized below.

Table 1: Culture and Capabilities for Each RMM Level

RMM Level	Use of Rules	Primary Goal of RMM Level	Comments
1	Re-orient or Re-discover (existing rules)	Knowledge of Rules	• Rules in business language • Rules tied to process models or use cases • Rules traced to systems implementation • Rules stored in spreadsheets
2	Re-act (to change)	Agility of Rules	• Rules in formal form possibly with rule authoring software • Glossary of terms tied to rules • Rules analyzable • Standard rule reports • Source rule repository with extensive traceability of rules to rule metadata, process models, object models, etc • Rules in agile technology (BRMS)
3	Re-align (with objectives)	Consistency and Alignment of Rules	• Rule sets assigned to business metrics • Rule sets shared as services across processes and systems • Business Rules Center of Excellence established • Possibly more than one BRMS • Standard methodology, templates, etc
4	Re-envision (short-term futures)	Future Predictions with Rules	• Potential events identified • Potential rules simulated • Revenue, profit, people differences estimated • Rules recast according to analysis
5	Re-invent (longer-term future)	Full Stewardship with Rules	• Rule stewards identified • Fast, first to define and respond • Ever-changing organization

The Rule Maturity Model and the Changing Relationship between Business and IT

Each higher level of the RMM, because there is more rigor in the methods and more sophistication in the software, offers the opportunity to re-shape the relationship between business and technical people. To understand how this relationship can evolve, let's first understand the basics of the business rule life cycle, which can provide a much shorter change cycle.

The concept of a business rule life cycle is new and it applies to all RMM Levels, except Level 0. In fact, for RMM Levels 1 through 5, the business rule life cycle is much the same. It usually consists of the following tasks or activities:

1. Document business objectives or requirements initially or requiring change.
2. Document business policies supporting the objective or requirement.
3. Identify source materials for underlying rules.
4. Discover and author rules in simple, business-friendly, natural language form (with glossary).
5. Author, validate, and analyze rules in rigorous, formal form with a semantic model of the underlying glossary.
6. Automate and test rules.
7. Simulate rules within a context.
8. Put rules into production.

A very significant difference among RMM Levels involves the role of business versus technical people in the business rule life cycle. At higher RMM Levels, businesspeople are able to carry out more of the steps in the business rule life cycle because there are methods, standards, and software that enable them to do so with minimal technical support.

What Happens Next-Technology Predictions in the Rule Maturity Model?

The incremental methodology and technology requirements for each level of the RMM are becoming well-known and widely accepted. Practitioners use the RMM to prepare for future technology advancements. Software vendors use the RMM to deliver on the promise of the Business Rules Approach.

Most recent advances include the interest in and addition of some business rule management support for non-technical users to BRMS products. Another important trend is that of Enterprise Decision Management (EDM), which takes advantage of BRMS technology and sometimes analytical models to improve operational decisions. Per Cutter Consortium[3], "EDM should be considered as a way to extend your organization's DW (data warehousing) and BI (business intelligence) capabilities by automating decisions through the use of rule-based systems and analytic modeling techniques."

For more insights into current technology trends and visions, see Chapter 15.

---

3. Hall, Curt, "Enterprise Decision Management: Business Intelligence Advisory Service," Executive Report volume 5, No. 6, Cutter Consortium

Summary and Future Vision

The RMM is a tested roadmap by which organizations set realistic business rule expectations and design a practical roadmap for getting there. The RMM keeps an organization grounded in a step-by-step Business Rules Approach that is customized to target business objectives. As such, the RMM is a guide for matching desired or required business benefits to the appropriate amount of investment in managing business rules. The RMM assists in defining the first steps in getting started while keeping a longer-term vision in sight.

Through the RMM, the vision of the Business Rules Approach will be realized:

To enable business leadership to take control of the guiding levers of the enterprise, and enable technology to match the rate of business change.

References

1. von Halle, Barbara, <u>Business Rules Applied</u> (2002: John Wiley & Sons, New York)
2. Hall, Curt, "Enterprise Decision Management: Business Intelligence Advisory Service," Executive Report volume 5, No. 6, Cutter Consortium

2 Business Rules Marketplace Today and Tomorrow: Based on a Maturity Survey

Barbara von Halle

Roots of the Business Rules Approach

The Business Rule Revolution is certainly not new, but it is quickly gaining momentum today. The Business Rule Revolution really has two parts: business rule *technology* revolution and business rule *methodology* revolution. Some aspects of the Business Rule technology revolution have existed for many decades, having beginnings in the technology of artificial intelligence and the discipline of knowledge engineering. The Business Rule technology revolution continues to benefit from advances delivered in business rule engines (today, often called business rule management systems or BRMS) that have been around and evolved over several decades. It also continues today with a new growing population of business rule engines (BRMS) in the OpenSource marketplace (where specific business rule engines are publicly available in part or in whole).

The recent Business Rule methodology revolution is also occurring today as practitioners integrate newly defined business rule deliverables into traditional requirements approaches and modeling techniques.

The methodology revolution is maturing to include emerging business rule standards and software tools for capturing business rules in business terms for business audiences and preparing the rules for automation. In some cases, business rule deliverables and corresponding tasks have been added to current familiar practices. Some methodology plug-ins for IBM® Rational Unified Process® or RUP® include business rule aspects. Some organizations have created a cross-reference from business rule deliverables to models developed using aspects of the Unified Modeling Language (UML).

Today, the methodology and technology roots of the Business Rule Revolution are colliding and integrating, giving prominence to the word "revolution." Given these various beginnings, where is the Business Rules Marketplace heading, and more importantly, what the current practices are in those areas? This chapter summarizes a survey of willing corporate and government organizations. It covers the following:

- Short-term purpose of the survey

- Longer-term purpose of the survey

- General background of participants

- 1. Industries

- 2. Point of contact for the survey

- 3. Business rule champion

- 4. Scope of Business Rules Approach

- 5. Major motivations for the Business Rules Approach

- 6. The need for good planning

- 7. Is a BRMS part of the solution?

- 8. Is a BPM or workflow product part of the solution?

- 9. Where are source rules stored?

- 10. Process for discovering rules
- 11. Current sources of rules
- 12. Anticipated or actual classifications of target rules
- 13. Desired software functionality
- 14. Common current states of rule maturity
- 15. Common target states of rule maturity
- Summary of the survey
- Lessons in the survey
- Reference to another survey

Short-term Purpose of the Survey

The immediate purpose of the survey is to establish a baseline of the Business Rules marketplace by documenting both the current and the future state of business rule practices based on an anonymous survey group. We also wanted to correlate current and target states to the KPI RMM™ levels. Doing so provides insight into the maturity of the marketplace and, more importantly, where it wants and needs to go in the near future.

Longer-term Purpose of the Survey

The longer-term goals of the survey are twofold. The first is to track the progress of the survey group over time to determine the economic impact of the Business Rules Approach as these organizations mature, and to determine the economic impact of the Business Rules Approach at each RMM level.

4. Scope of Business Rules Approach

It was important to understand the intended scope of the Business Rules Approach and corresponding business rule management. Differences in scope (e.g., small pilot, first project, across a business unit, entire enterprise) imply differences in organizational change and business rule management software.

All but a small exception of the participating organizations indicated that the scope of their Business Rules Approach, at the time of the survey, was limited to one project. An outlier was starting out with an enterprise approach, establishing first an enterprise methodology, standards, and a center of excellence.

However, in half of the organizations the goal beyond a successful project was to extend the approach to a business unit perspective, or enterprise-wide. These organizations wanted to learn lessons from a pilot or project before leveraging methods, techniques, standards, roles, and software on a broader scale.

5. Major Motivations for the Business Rules Approach

The major motivations for investing in the Business Rules Approach were not surprising to KPI. The list below indicates the motivations, starting with the most to the least popular. Organizations were invited to provide multiple motivations, if appropriate.

- **Agility**: More than half of the participants indicated agility as a major motivation. Likewise, such organizations tended to deploy a BRMS as part of their technology solution.

- **Consistency**: Surprisingly, consistency and reusability of rule sets surfaced as the second most popular motivation, as 50% of the participants cited it as a major motivator.

- **Business Control or Empowerment**: The idea of the business people being closer to authoring, testing, and discussing rules was the third popular motivation, earning votes from 30% of the organizations.

- **Knowledge Retention**: The need to document or manage a central rule repository due to retirement of employees or outsourcing of development came in fourth. It earned votes from about 20% of the participants. However, since the survey, this motivation has surfaced more frequently as the working population ages. KPI suspects this motivation is more critical today than at the time of the survey.

- **Legacy Renewal**: The desire to modernize legacy systems was cited in only one case. However, this is likely a subtle motivation as the need for agility, consistency, business empowerment, or knowledge retention implies legacy renewal and the Business Rules Approach.

Compliance was originally expected to be a top motivation, but did not take a prominent role at the time of KPI's survey. The reason for its lack of prominence may be that organizations needed time to absorb and translate the meaning of new compliance regulations (e.g., Sarbanes-Oxley). Initial compliance endeavors focused on understanding and documenting critical business processes first. The need to document detailed rules behind the processes came later.

Not on this list, but mentioned often by contributors to this book, is the motivation to build a stronger partnership between the business and IT. None of the survey participants listed this motivation as a critical one; yet, for organizations with more experience in the

Business Rules Approach, this result was highlighted as the most significant benefit. This was true for at least one participant that did not even deploy a BRMS.

6. The Need for Good Planning

Because the participants were already started on their Business Rules Approach, KPI asked them to expose those areas needing extra attention so as to manage the revolution gracefully.

By far, the most common area needing good planning was the management of change. Over 80% of the organizations listed this as the most critical item. This area included considerations such as understanding the time it takes to absorb new skills, allowing enough time to evaluate BRMS, allowing ample time to consider a source rule repository, dealing with resistance to change, encouraging the value of sharing rules and stewardship, providing guidance on a reasonable evolution of business versus IT relationships, and enabling positive collaboration.

About 30% of organizations also listed rule management issues as needing ample planning. These included defining a full business rule life cycle (from source documents or people to source rule repository to simulation and testing to deployment) and the impact of having lost the old rules. The latter surfaced as the unexpected realization that no one actually knew the old rules, in systems or in manual processes, so additional time was needed to re-discover them or invent new ones. Another important item was to provide training and ample time for rule authors to write rules consistently. A lack of standards for some of the rule-related deliverables, requiring organization-specific standards, was mentioned.

About 20% of participants cited technology issues that need attention. These ranged from the time it takes to learn new technology (BRMS) to the time it takes to implement rules in old technology (COBOL). It also included the time to find a source rule repository.

7. Is a BRMS Part of the Solution?

Most of the organizations included a BRMS as a critical part of the solution. This makes sense, since most organizations also listed agility as a motivating factor and are aiming for RMM Level 2. A few organizations indicated the need for more than one kind of BRMS, and most of them had already selected their chosen product; only a few had not selected a product. One organization was not sure whether it needed a BRMS.

8. Is a BPM or Workflow Product Part of the Solution?

Approximately 65% of participants indicated that a BPM or workflow product is to be part of their solution, with the rest indicating that this was not so. Most of them, however, had not selected the BPM or workflow product of their choice.

This was interesting because the integration issues between BPM and BRMS technology did not appear to be high priority or of great concern to this group.

9. Where Are Source Rules Stored?

It was important to explore where organizations are storing the business rules for the business audience, how they are making the rules accessible, and how they are managing changes over time by business people. The results were not surprising to KPI, but still disappointing. The results demonstrate the need for better available software for managing source rules (which are the rules as the business person knows them). The answers to this question were so varied that only Microsoft Excel spreadsheets stood out as the most common, with fewer than 30% of the organizations using spreadsheets.

There was an outlier documenting rules simply in the documentation for the legacy code. In a similar vein, another stored them in the BRMS. About 15% of the organizations built a home-grown rule repository, 21 % stored such rules in a requirements tool, and 15% did so in extensions to a modeling tool. Other organizations were not specific about whether these rules were stored anywhere or even managed after they were implemented in target technology.

10. Process for Discovering Rules

One survey question asked participants to explain their rule discovery process, specifically, what their starting point for finding rules was and what other pieces they anchor those rules to. Their responses are, in order of popularity:

- **Use Cases**: Almost every participating organization utilized use cases as a starting point for soliciting rules and organizing them for action.

- **Process Models**: Most participants also utilized a process modeling technique as a starting point for harvesting business rules. These models included process maps, activity diagrams, and IDEF0 diagrams (one method for modeling decisions, actions, and activities of an organization or system).

- **Documents**: Approximately 35% of the participants started with documents, such as process descriptions, policy manuals, or legal documents. Therefore, their rule discovery processes involved scanning documents, highlighting sentences resembling rules, building a glossary, and rewriting rules.

- **Code**: About 20% of the participants started with program code. These organizations deployed business rule mining techniques to find rules there.

11. Current Sources of Rules

To learn where rules live in these organizations today, we explored the most common rule sources. Each participant could list multiple sources. These turned out to be:

- **People**: More than 50% of the participants indicated that rules are best obtained from people in the organization, either because these people are experts or they are retiring. This indicates that rule harvesting techniques through interviewing or facilitated sessions are very valuable in most places, along with rule authoring training and software.

- **Code:** Also half of the participants indicated that a majority of rules are truly buried in program code. Therefore, business rule mining from code methods and tools are valuable.

- **Documents**: Half of the participants indicated that rules are buried in documents.

12. Anticipated or Actual Classifications of Target Rules

KPI wanted to learn whether there was a natural distinction among organizations as to specific types of rules. Organizations could list more than one classification of rules that they anticipated managing.

Across the participants, there emerged a distinct separation of target rules into two groups.

One group of rules was defined as simple to complex constraint and validation rules. These are the kinds of rules that guide typical transactions through their life cycles, such as rules relating to totaling dollar amounts, validating a customer, and verifying delivery on a product to a location at a particular time. These are rules that, in the past, have not been implemented in special rule technology, but were embedded in home-grown code. These tend to be simple and unconnected rules that validate various parts of a form, for example, or of data entered through a web page.

Another group of rules was defined as complex inferencing rules for decision making. These are the kinds of rules that involve complicated, interrelated judgments based on many conditions and interim conclusions. These include determining a credit score or determining which students receive how much tuition assistance. These are the kinds of rules that historically have benefited from deployment in commercial or home-grown BRMS.

These different groups of rules have different characteristics: the latter voluminous with interrelated conditions and conclusions whereas the former tend to be fewer in number, simpler, and not necessarily related to each other. Each group may be better served by technology specific to its unique characteristics.

Only a few participants indicated that complex computations or formulas were the prevalent classification of rules they sought to manage better.

13. Desired Software Functionality

Each participating organization was asked to rank software functionality according to how critical that functionality was to the success of their business rule endeavors.

Below is a list of the functionality that was ranked as "high" by at least one participating organization. They are ranked from the functionality having the most "high" votes to the one having the least number of "high" votes. Votes of "medium" or "low" priority are not included.

- **Automated Rule Analysis** (the ability to detect conflicting, overlapping, and incomplete rule sets): This requirement yielded the highest votes, as over 60% of the participating organizations considered automatic rule analysis versus manual inspection to be critical, especially when non-technical people may be authoring rules.

- **Single Generation of Executable Code** (the ability to generate code from a rule expression to one target automation platform): 50% of the organizations ranked this as a high priority, mostly because they had selected one BRMS product.

- **Automatic Workflow for Rule Management** (the ability to manage roles, queues, and deliverables along the full rule change life cycle): It was a surprise that almost 50% of the organizations rated this as a "high" priority, yet KPI knows of no commercial offering for this specific functionality.

- **Multiple Generation of Executable Code** (the ability to generate code from a rule expression to more than one target automation platform):

Almost 30% of participants rated this a "high" priority, indicating that these organizations are thinking into the future, at RMM Level 3 or above.

- **Integration of Rule Authoring Software with Other Tools** (the ability to trace rules and rule sets to deliverables in requirements tools and modeling tools): Only 7% of participants ranked this requirement as "high," although most organizations indicated that they either lacked such tools, were not using them, or had not selected them yet.

- **Update of Rules in Production** (the ability for non-technical business people to make rule changes directly to production systems): Only one outlier considered this "high." Instead, most organizations are aiming for business people to have more control over specifying the rules, determining the impact of changing the rules, and testing the rules. However, it was not usually the case that these organizations had a desire for such people to make changes in production systems. More important is the need for rule changes to occur quickly (faster than changes to other kinds of requirements). However, these changes can be made by technical support people, as long as the changes occur correctly and quickly. In a rare instance, businesspeople have the ability to change rules, analyze them for errors, and test and simulate them for impact analysis, but they do not want or need the capability to deploy the changed rules in production.

14. Common Current States of Rule Maturity

At this point in the history of this ongoing survey, KPI determined, based on the answers to the survey questions, the RMM level of each organization at the time of the survey and their ultimate goal. These RMM levels would likely explain the answers to the questions and provide guidance to readers.

At the time of the survey, the participants fell into two groups regarding where they started in their RMM journey. One-third of the participants were starting at RMM Level 2. These are the organizations that, long ago, deployed either a home-grown or commercial BRMS and built a support group around it. These organizations had established centralized business rule engine groups, but the connection to and participation by business people was not high. Today, these participating organizations are looking to be better at managing the business-side of the business rules and bringing the business experts closer to the process.

Two-thirds of the participants were starting at RMM Level 0, which is where KPI finds most organizations today. In fact, this group is growing and represents the organizations that have not previously deployed special rule technology. Today they are interested in separating the business rules from business process models, use cases, other requirements, and, perhaps, but not necessarily, deploying rule-specific technology.

So, where did the participants want to be?

13. The most desired software functionality among participants is automated rule analysis, generation of executable code to one target platform, and automatic workflow for the business rule life cycle.

14. The most common starting point for participants is RMM Level 0.

15. The most common target state for participants is RMM Level 2. Higher levels of the RMM are achievable, but rare today. Achieving RMM Level 3 usually requires home-grown software. Therefore, more software advances are needed and expected for enabling rule management and authoring by the business's true business rule stewards.

Next Steps for the Survey

We will increase the survey participants and continue to evolve the survey questions as long as it provides value to the Business Rule Revolution.

Reference to Another Survey

Readers may want to refer to another survey that assesses the business rules marketplace, whose conclusions are similar to those in this chapter. A white paper on that survey is "Business Rules Market Adoption Survey Results" by Michael Peters of Whitespace Consulting and it can be found at http://www.lambert-tech.com/documents/BusinessRul esMarketAdoptionSurvey_Results_Whitespace.pdf

Another document on Best Practices is at http://www.lambert-tech.com/documents/BusinessRul esMarketAdoption_BestPractices_Whitespace.pdf

A related presentation can be found at http://www.lambert-tech.com/documents/210004_La mbertBethune.pdf.

3 Enterprise Architecture: Managing Complexity and Change

John A. Zachman

Introduction

It is my perception that enterprise architecture presently is a grossly misunderstood concept among management, probably for several reasons. The principal reason likely is that enterprise architecture is seen to be an information technology, or systems issue, not a management issue. Enterprise architecture tends to surface in the enterprise through the information systems community, and the information systems people seem to have some skills to do enterprise architecture if any enterprise architecture is being done or is to be done in the enterprise.

However, the origins of the concept come from Robert Anthony, "Planning and Control Systems, A Framework for Analysis"[4]; Jay Forrester, "Industrial Dynamics"[5]; Erich Helfert, "Techniques of Financial Analysis"[6]; Peter Drucker, "The Practice of Management"[7]; George Steiner, "Comprehensive

---

4. Robert Anthony, *Planning and Control Systems, A Framework for Analysis*. Cambridge, MA: Harvard University Press, 1965.
5. Jay Forester, *Industrial Dynamics*. Boston: Massachusetts Institute of Technology Press, 1961.
6. Erich Helfert. *Techniques of Financial Analysis*. New York: Dow-Jones Irwin, 1962.

Managerial Planning"[8];and more recently, Peter Senge, "The Fifth Discipline"[9] to name but a few. These works have nothing to do with information technology or information related issues per se. The basic concept of enterprise architecture is that it is important to understand the enterprise first, before attempting to overlay infrastructure investments required to support the enterprise and to facilitate its on-going change, because unless engineered correctly, infrastructure (including information systems) tends to be extremely costly and resistant to change.

Reviewing Alvin Toffler's books about change, first, "Knowledge is change... and accelerating knowledge-acquisition, fueling the great engine of technology, means accelerating change."[10] The rate of change is increasing dramatically and putting extreme pressure on reducing time-to-market to accommodate the rapid change. Second, the Industrial Age was different from the Agricultural Age and the Information Age is different from the Industrial Age.[11] The implication of this is that the game has changed —dramatically. Third, if you give everyone access to the same information at the same time, the power will shift outward in the enterprise.[12] No longer will power be concentrated in two or three people at the top who know everything, decide everything, and control everything. In fact, if the customer (or recipient of the product or service) of the enterprise has access to the same information that the enterprise has access to, the power will shift into the customer environment. It will become "market-driven."

The practical implications of these observations are first, the complexity of the enterprise will continue to escalate. The moment you say, "customer relationship management," or "one-on-one

7. Peter Drucker. *The Practice of Management.* New York: Harper & Row, 1954.
8. George Steiner. *Comprehensive Managerial Planning.* The Planning Executives Institute, 1972.
9. Peter Senge. *The Fifth Discipline.* New York: Doubleday, 1990.
10. Alvin Toffler. *Future Shock.* New York: Random House, 1970.
11. Alvin Toffler. *The Third Wave.* New York: William Morrow and Company, 1980.
12. Alvin Toffler. *Powershift.* New York: Bantam Books, 1990.

marketing," or "a market of one," etc., you are signing up for orders-of-magnitude increases in complexity. That is, the day you have to treat each customer as an individual, rather than as a group, a segment, or a type, you are talking about major increases in complexity.

This chapter discusses the following:

- The changing enterprise concept

- Increased complexity in the Information Age

- The Zachman Framework for Enterprise Architecture

- A framework metaphor

- The Zachman Framework and Business Rules

- Conclusion

- References

The Changing Enterprise Concept

This is a fundamental change in the Industrial Age concept of the enterprise. In the Industrial Age, the basic idea was to get a good product or service and then find a lot of customers to sell it to. That is, from the perspective of the enterprise, the market, the customers), were integrated. By default, the customer had to deal with the complexity of "integration" of the enterprise products or services. In contrast, the basic idea of the Information Age is to find a good customer and then identify and provide whatever products or services are required to keep that customer a good customer. That is, from the perspective of the customer, the enterprise products have to be integrated. In the case of services, it is the enterprise itself that has to be integrated. In the Information Age case, it is the Enterprise that has to deal with the complexity of integration. If the "Powershift"[13] takes place (which I am sure it will take place if you want to stay in the new, Information Age game), the burden of integration will transfer to the supplier. The customer wants to see the enterprise products and/or the enterprise itself customized to the interest of the customer.

Another practicality of the changing game is reduced time-to-market. That is, there will be less and less time from the moment the enterprise receives an order until it fulfills the order for a product or service customized for the customer. As the rate of change continues to escalate, the time-to-market for whatever the enterprise produces will tend to shrink. In fact, if the rate of change goes to infinity, the time-to-market will go to zero. This is the case where the customer is unable to define the characteristics of the product or service they have to take delivery on until the point in time that they have to take delivery.

---

13. *Ibid.*

From an information technology perspective, the practical implication of extreme complexity and extremely high rates of change is that the enterprise will be unable to define the characteristics of the implementation they need to take delivery on until the point in time they need to take delivery. The requirement will be for enterprise-wide, integrated implementations for immediate delivery.

Increased Complexity in the Information Age

The business-significant characteristics of the Information Age are dramatic escalation of complexity and dramatic escalation of the rate of change. The management question is: how will you deal with orders-of-magnitude increases in complexity and orders-of-magnitude increases in the rate of change? In seven thousand years of known history, the only device humanity has come up with so far to deal with complexity and change is *architecture*.

First, regarding complexity, if it (whatever "it" is) gets so complex, you can't remember everything about it at one time, you have to learn how to describe it before you can create it. If somebody hadn't figured out how to describe buildings, we would still be living in log cabins. If somebody hadn't figured out how to describe automobiles, we'd still be riding around on horses. If somebody hadn't figured out how to describe airplanes, we'd still be traveling in covered wagons. If somebody hadn't figured out how to describe computers, we'd still be using an abacus or adding up columns of numbers with pencils and paper. And so on. In the Industrial Age, we learned that there is a set of descriptive representations required to describe a complex industrial product including, among other things, drawings, functional specifications, bills-of-material, etc., that is, *architecture*.

Regarding change, once you create a complex product and want to change it, you start with the architecture: the drawings, the functional specifications, the bills of materials, etc. If you have no architecture and you want to change something (e.g. a building, airplane, computer, etc.), there are only three possible options: 1) You can change it by trial and error and see what happens. This is the high-risk option in that you could make a rather small change and potentially cause irreparable damage. 2) You can reverse- engineer the architecture, the drawings, the functional specifications, the bills of material, etc. to serve as a basis for changing it. That takes time and costs money. 3) Or, you could scrap the whole thing and start over again, building a new, changed version. The point is, architecture is the baseline for changing anything that is already in existence. If you have no architecture, you will have to create or re-create the architecture or risk scrapping the product.

In the Industrial Age it was the industrial products that were increasing in complexity and changing. If we, humanity, had not figured out how to describe complex industrial products, we still would be in the Industrial Age and we would not have Boeing 747's, hundred-story buildings, ocean liners, supercomputers, etc. It has only been in the last fifty years or so that we have figured out how to exploit these very sophisticated descriptive representations of industrial products to produce custom products, mass-produced in quantities of one for immediate delivery. This idea of "mass-customization" is still relatively new even in manufacturing, however; as the Information Age wears on and customers want (or need) their products to be integrated to their unique requirements in very short periods of time, mass-customization will likely be the rule, not an exception for industrial products and for enterprises.

In the Information Age, it is not only the industrial product that is increasing in complexity and changing, it is the *enterprise* that is increasing in complexity and the *enterprise* that is changing. The question for the

Information Age is: what is architecture relative to enterprises? This may well be *the* issue of the century.[14]

The Zachman Framework for Enterprise Architecture

If you (the enterprise) do not have an enterprise architecture strategy, you likely don't have a strategy for addressing orders-of-magnitude increases in complexity and orders-of-magnitude increases in the rate of change. The author is confident that complexity and change will be the characteristics of the Information Age, and "the enterprises that can accommodate the concepts of enterprise architecture are likely to be the survivors and those that don't are likely to be the rest."[15]

I spent more than 35 years of my professional life trying to figure out what Architecture looks like relative to enterprises. If I have done anything of value, my contribution has been in the form of a framework, a Framework for Enterprise Architecture. The Framework for Enterprise Architecture simply defines what enterprise architecture looks like. It is not mysterious how I figured this out. I went back to the Industrial Age products and tried to understand what Architecture was relative to industrial products, and then I simply assigned enterprise names to the set of design artifacts that were created for describing anything, including enterprises.

It turns out that architecture is architecture is architecture. It doesn't matter what the architecture is for: buildings, airplanes, automobiles, computers, whatever. The underlying order of the descriptive representations is the same. This is a very, very brief

---

14. John A. Zachman, "Enterprise Architecture: The Issue of the Century." *Database Programming and Design Magazine,* Volume 10, number 3 (1997).
15. *Ibid.*

discussion of a very complex subject.[16] In fact, I have written an entire book[17] on this subject. For the purposes of this article, the descriptive representations (the architecture) fall into a two-dimensional classification system:

The Interrogative dimension, a single abstraction of:

WHAT the product is made of: the material composition, the parts that must be in inventory to create the product, the bill-of-materials

HOW the product works: the transformation of raw material and energy, the functional specifications

WHERE the parts are located relative to one another: the geometry, the drawings

WHO does what work: the operating instructions

WHEN do things happen: the machine cycles, the timing diagrams

WHY do they happen: the engineering design objectives

The audience dimension, a single audience for whom each interrogative is framed:

SCOPE – setting the boundary, the limits of each abstraction

OWNER – the needed concepts of the end result, the requirements

---

16. Boeing 747's are complex and architecture for Boeing 747's is complex. Enterprises are even more complex than Boeing 747's and therefore enterprise architecture is going to be a very complex subject. People tend not to want to hear that Enterprises are complex but I would be less than honest if I didn't point this out. The whole reason for engineering anything is to make whatever you are engineering as simple as possible … but no simpler. (I think it was Einstein that said that.)
17. John A. Zachman, *The Zachman Framework: A Primer for Enterprise Engineering and Manufacturing.*. La Cañada, CA: Zachman International, 2003. http://www.ZachmanInternational.com.

DESIGNER – the systematic logic to realize the concepts, the schematics

BUILDER – the technology constructs to build the product, the blueprints

SUB-CONTRACTOR – the production tool configuration for the components

OPERATOR – the end result – this is no longer architecture (that is, a description) – it is an instance of the product, the end result

This two-dimensional classification system is typically depicted as a "framework" with the interrogatives (abstractions) appearing as the columns and the audience perspectives appearing as the rows. Since each column (interrogative) is unique and varies independently from all the other columns and since each row is unique and varies independently from the row above and from the row below, the framework, the "Zachman Framework," is NOT simply a matrix. It is a "normalized" schema. Only one fact can go in one cell, that is, one "meta-entity" can only be classified in a single cell.[18]

Although I learned about the underlying schema empirically by looking at the engineering design artifacts, the descriptive representations of Industrial Age products, my interest was in enterprise architecture, so I simply assigned enterprise names to the same engineering design artifacts that were relevant for describing airplanes, buildings, computers, anything. Figure 3[19] is the Framework for Enterprise Architecture, the "Zachman Framework" as it presently is depicted.

---

18. For the non-technical reader, you don't have to be intimidated by the words "schema," "normalization" or "meta-entity." The "schema" is just a two dimensional classification system that can be depicted in a matrix form, rows and columns. "Normalization" simply means that the classification system is "clean"—that is, there are no "apples and oranges" or mixtures in any cell of the matrix. And, "meta-entity" is an abstraction that you need if you want to store something in a database. In the case of enterprise architecture, you *will* want to store the models in a database .

19. The original version of this framework is available at www.ZachmanInternational.com/fwgraphic.html.

The meta-entities and the meta-meta-entities have appeared at the bottom of each cell of the Framework since its inception. I have changed some of the words since I first created the graphic around 1980, but the schema itself has not changed; nor will it ever change. In fact, the classification on either axis of the Framework has been employed by humanity unchanged for hundreds if not thousands of years. There are two reasons for my changes of some, actually few, of the words in the graphic. First, our understanding of the schema in 1980 was limited, and some of the words I selected did not accurately represent the classification concepts. Second, and unfortunately, I came from the information community, and some of the words I selected came from my information systems vocabulary.[20] This has contributed to some of the misunderstanding of enterprise architecture as an information technology issue, as opposed to the correct understanding that it is an enterprise issue.

---

20. We have been working with some linguists from SIL International for nearly five years to identify words that more accurately convey the concepts of the framework schema and to employ words that are more business-oriented than technology-oriented. In November, 2005, we published the new standard meta model for the framework at www.ZachmanInternational.com. Although the new standards are available at no cost, they are distributed on a CD that contains my book, among other things. The CD must be registered to be opened.

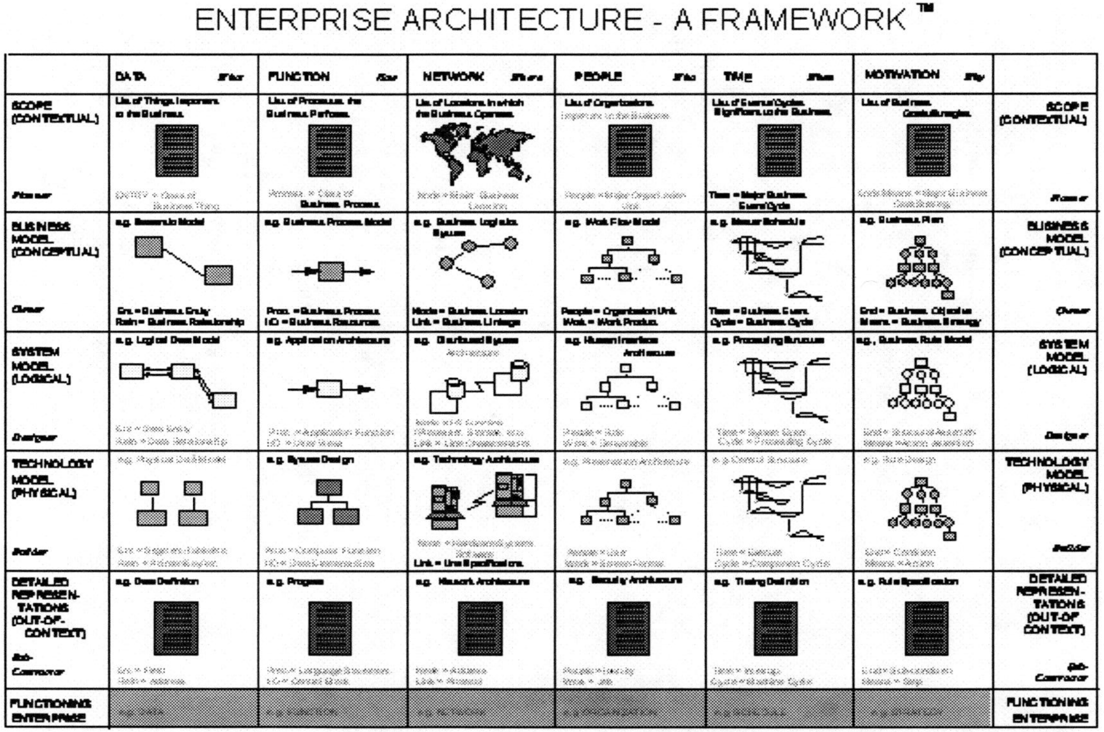

ENTERPRISE ARCHITECTURE - A FRAMEWORK ™

Figure 3: The Framework for Enterprise Architecture (the "Zachman Framework").

Since each cell of the Framework is unique and since it can contain only two meta- entities, the meta-entity that constitutes the focus of the cell description and its relationship with itself (the other meta-entity), I call each instance of a cell model a "primitive" model. The raw material for doing engineering is the engineering design artifacts for the complex product. For engineering an enterprise, the Framework cell descriptions, the primitive models, are the raw material for doing enterprise engineering. In fact, I would observe, if there are no primitive models for any given enterprise, that enterprise has not been engineered. It has simply happened.

In contrast, implementations require components from more than one cell: composite models as opposed to primitive models. A primitive model is not implementable. A composite model is made up of components from more than one primitive model. Implementation is manufacturing, not engineering. Primitive models are for engineering; composite models are for manufacturing.

A Framework Metaphor

Maybe a useful metaphor for the Framework is the Periodic Table. It was around 1890 that Mendeleyev published the Periodic Table, a two-dimensional classification of the chemical elements of the universe. The Periodic Table classified all of the possible elements even though many of the elements had not yet been discovered. The elements themselves do not exist as elements in nature. In nature, the elements only exist as compounds, that is, as composites of more than one element. The elements of the Periodic Table are the raw material for doing chemical engineering. Chemical engineering is creating compounds, but *not* manufacturing. Before Mendeleyev defined the Periodic Table, there were chemicals (compounds), but there was no "chemistry." Nothing was predictable or repeatable except by personal experience. The enterprise framework implications of this analogy are that although the enterprise is made up of composite implementations, they were not likely engineered. They were created by trial and error based on the experience of the implementers.

If you assume the most robust case, that there is a many-to-many relationship[21] between any one meta-entity in any one cell and all the other meta-entities in the row, as well as a many-to-many relationship between any one meta-entity and the meta-entities of the cell above and the cell below, and if you had populated a data base with primitive models for some enterprise, then you could create virtually any composite implementation for that enterprise simply by binding the primitive components together. That is, you could "mass-customize" the enterprise at the click of a mouse. You could satisfy the demand for virtually any enterprise-wide implementation at the point in time the enterprise discovered they needed that implementation.

Please remember that this is a very brief discussion of a very complex subject, and that it will likely take some period of time to accumulate some (and possibly someday, all) of the primitive models. However, hopefully this gives you a sense of the enterprise possibility for addressing orders of magnitude increases in complexity and orders of magnitude increase in the rate of change, by engineering the enterprise (the primitive models) and assembling the enterprise to order (building composites) on demand.

---

21. For those non-technical readers, a many-to-many relationship simply means that there are two different things that are related to one another but that vary independently from one another, such as employees and positions. They are different, and they are related, but they vary independently.

The Zachman Framework and Business Rules

At the time I published the second IBM Systems Journal article on my Framework in 1992,[22] we felt that business rules were classified in the *Why* column (Column 6) and the *System* row (Row 3). In fact, I named the column 6, row 3 cell "e.g. Business Rule Model." Subsequent to that publication, we have learned much about primitives and composites as well as about business rules. Today, I would observe that the focus for identifying and defining the business rules may well still be column 6, row 3, but the business rules themselves are likely complex composite constructs relating meta-entities from more than one cell. Had we known what we know today when the GUIDE Business Rules Project Final Report was published in October, 1997[23], we probably could have anticipated the composite nature of the business rules simply by observing the meta-model described in the report. Clearly, there were meta-entities that would be classified in cells other than simply column 6, row 3. Further, the row 2 Business Rules meta-model that was published in the October, 2000 report by the Business Rules Group in "Organizing Business Plans: The Standard Model for Business Rule Motivation" also included meta-entities that would be classified in Columns and Rows other than and in addition to column 6, row 2. The body of knowledge in enterprise architecture, as well as in business rules, is presently exploding. There is no better time than now to be involved in these vital enterprise issues.

---

22. J.F. Sowa and J.A. Zachman, "Extending and Formalizing the Framework for Information Systems Architecture," *IBM Systems Journal*, vol. 31, no. 3, (1992).
23. Both Barbara von Halle and I were contributors to the report *GUIDE Business Rules project. Final Report. Revision 1.2.* October 1997. The project likely spanned more than five years and was probably the first formal publication on the subject of Business Rules.

Conclusion

I don't think there is any question about whether an enterprise is going to do enterprise architecture or not; that is, it will not be optional if an enterprise intends to be viable in the Information Age. The only question is when they will start working on enterprise architecture, because there potentially is a lot of work to do—and at the point in time the Enterprise is going to need it, it is going to be too late to do it! Business rules may well be a good place to start working on it.

References

Anthony, Robert. *Planning and Control Systems, A Framework for Analysis.* Cambridge, MA: Harvard University Press, 1965.

Drucker, Peter. *The Practice of Management.* New York: Harper & Row, 1954.

Forrester, Jay. *Industrial Dynamics.* Boston: Massachusetts Institute of Technology Press, 1961.

Helfert, Erich. *Techniques of Financial Analysis.* New York: Dow-Jones Irwin, 1962.

Senge, Peter. *The Fifth Discipline.* New York: Doubleday, 1990.

Steiner, George. *Comprehensive Managerial Planning.* The Planning Executives Institute, 1972

Toffler, Alvin. *Future Shock.* New York: Random House, 1970.

Toffler, Alvin. *Powershift.* New York: Bantam Books, 1970.

Toffler, Alvin. *The Third Wave.* New York: William Morrow and Company, 1970.

Zachman, John A. *The Zachman Framework: A Primer for Enterprise Engineering and Manufacturing.* La Cañada, CA: Zachman International, 2003. http://www.ZachmanInternational.com.

Zachman, John A. "Enterprise Architecture: The Issue of the Century." *Database Programming and Design Magazine*, 3 (1997).

4 The Business Architecture of Business Rules Based Enterprises

Larry Goldberg

"An architecture is a framework for the disciplined introduction of change." (de Marco, "On Systems Architecture", The Atlantic Guild, Inc. 1995)

Introduction

"Business rules...serve as the guidance system that influences the collective behavior of an organization's people and information systems. The *Business Rules Approach* is a formal way of managing and automating and organization's business rules so that the business behaves and evolves as its leaders intend."[24]   But, once an organization has determined to pursue the Business Rules Approach, what are the architectural implications of that decision? If the Business Rules Approach is indeed a "formal way of managing and automating" enterprise solutions, then no doubt a reference architecture for the design of these solutions exists. Or does it?

There is little published material on the subject. In fact, what formalized architecture for business rules that does exist is principally provided by Business

24. Barbara von Halle, *Business Rules Applied* (New York: John Wiley & Sons), 2002

Rule Management System (BRMS) vendors. As such, it is focused on patterns appropriate to specific technology—and for the most part it focuses on technical deployment rather than the business aspects. Here we have the unfortunate, but common, specter of architecture being driven by technology—not an unknown phenomenon in this industry, but nevertheless an undesirable practice. Therefore, this chapter covers the following:

- Business rules in the context of business enterprise architecture
- A brief discussion of the KPI RMM and its impact on architecture
- The rule authoring and governance environment
- The rule design environment
- The rule deployment environment
- A brief—but important—digression from architecture
- Returning to the architectural considerations in the design environment
- Deployment environment
- A special problem: business rules versus business process management
- Conclusion

Business Rules in the Context of Business Enterprise Architecture

To consider suitable patterns for a business rules architecture, it is important to start within the context of an accepted business enterprise architecture framework. The choice may be any one of the accepted models (they map well to one another). This chapter starts with the Zachman Framework (ZFW) because of its elegance and simplicity. It is conveniently described in Figure 3 of Chapter 3 by its author, John Zachman.

In this framework, the architecture of the business enterprise is fully represented in a series of columns and rows.

The six columns represent the "what, how, where, who, when, and why" of the enterprise. Five rows represent the views of the enterprise, and the sixth is the actual functioning enterprise. "The perspectives or rows are very abstract ... near the top, but become progressively more ... (technical) toward the bottom until an implementation emerges on the last row. This implies that the perspectives can be mapped to a product development life cycle where the top rows are used early on while the bottom rows become more important during the latter phases...The top two rows are intensively business-oriented and can be expressed in business-oriented vocabularies, while the bottom four rows are in the technical domain."[25]

This view of the enterprise is complete and the rows and columns remain in constant orthogonal balance. It clearly shows the independence of business rules (column 6, or ZFW C6) to conventional system requirements (ZFW C1, C2, and C3). It also illustrates how business rules authorship should appropriately be performed in rows 1, 2 and 3, (ZFW R1, R2, R3) system design should take place in ZFW R4, and deployment should occur in ZFW R5 and R6.

It is important to understand that while the framework may be used at the enterprise level, it may also be recursed to lower levels of the enterprise to describe business units, organizations, and even individual projects within the larger enterprise, each constrained within the bounds specified at the higher level. This is key to understanding the opportunity of re-use of business rules across the enterprise as rules architectures approach the highest levels of the KPI Rule Maturity Model (RMM).

---

25. Larry Goldberg, "Architecture," Systems and Software Consortium, 2005

A Brief Discussion of the KPI RMM and its Impact on Architecture

KPI's Rule Maturity Model (KPI RMM™) is a framework that organizations use to determine and improve their ability to develop, evolve, and align business policies and business rules in a rapidly-changing or highly-regulated business environment. (A detailed explanation of the RMM is in Chapter 1).

The RMM is a model for organizational improvement. It is aimed at the business process of managing core business policies and rules from business inception to deployment, which may include automation of business rules in software. The maturity levels are based upon the quality improvements in the business' management and awareness of the business process around rules management, rather than the quality of the software. We refer to levels of maturity as RMM1, RMM2, RMM3 and so on.

In a real sense, the KPI RMM™ is a roadmap toward the goal of achieving realization of the full promise of the Business Rules Approach.

An Architectural Approach to Business Rules

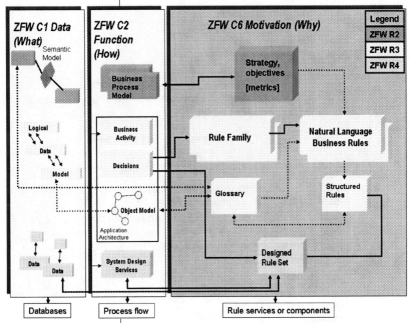

Figure 4: A Business Rules Model Mapped to the Zachman Framework

As indicated in the ZFW, business rules originate from and are subject to business objectives and motivations, whether these are internal or external (such as regulations). From an architectural point of view, some of the key characteristics of rules are:

- Rules are present in many forms throughout the business. Often they are not even recorded, but simply understood.

- There is a class of rules that are subject to a high frequency of change. The volatility of these dynamic business rules is believed to have increased in recent years, and is considered to be generally significantly greater than the rate of change of business systems requirements.

- Certain rules are frequently required to be verified and validated by outside regulatory or audit bodies, as to:

  - Content

  - Execution

  - Result

- Rules may be both automated in technology and manually executed —in some cases the same rules can be found in both environments.

- When rules are automated, they are often deployed in many, if not all, layers of an n-tier architecture, frequently in disparate technologies.

- When automated, business rules are expressed in completely different terms and language from how they exist in the business domain. Frequently a single business rule will translate into many lines of code in a designed rule set of "technical" rules.

These characteristics point to a need for separation of rules authoring environments from the design and the deployment environments. The authoring is essentially a business activity, while the design is technology constrained and focused on the implementation of those rules within one or more target technologies.

Happily, this is consistent with the Zachman Framework. Consider the three layers of architecture in the Business Rules Approach, and discuss their relationship to the Zachman Framework:

The Rule Authoring and Governance Environment

This is analogous to the first three rows of the Zachman framework, where we capture:

- business goals and their motivations (row 1, Contextual),

- business rules (row 2, Conceptual), and

- authored rules in a comprehensive rule model (row 3, Logical).

This implies the relationship of the business strategy and other business-based constraints to their related business rules. It occurs in such a way that the rules will immediately be highlighted when the prescribed business motivations change.

The authoring environment provides the tools for the gathering (also referred to as harvesting) of rules from their sources. This may be a bottom-up process to discover the rules that are in place in existing systems or practices, or it may be a top-down process deriving the rules from policies or new business directions.

The sources may include rule mining artifacts (via tools and manual methods), interviews, document examinations, and similar discovery items.

This environment is independent of the design and deployment environment, because it is an activity that is business-focused and must necessarily be available to the business. Ultimately (at the higher levels of RMM), the authoring of rules should be managed and led by the business.

The primary tools used in this environment include rule-mining or legacy-understanding tools, business and process modeling tools, and most importantly, a Source Rule Repository (SRR) which serves as the central store of and access to the business rules, their models and glossary for the business audience.

The most important characteristic of a SRR is its ability to be independent of and agnostic to the systems deploying those rules, and to their design and architecture. Depending on the level of maturity required, the SRR should provide features that permit comprehensive business management functions to be performed on the business rules. The extent of functionality is driven by the target state of KPI RMM™ desired. Figure 5 is a starting point for correlating RMM levels and ZFW rows to corresponding SRR capabilities.

	RMM 1	RMM 2	RMM 3	RMM 4	RMM 5
ZFW R2: Resources to be Managed	Strategy, Objectives and Policy Documents	Strategy, Objectives and Policy Documents	Strategy, Objectives and Policy Documents	Strategy, Objectives and Policy Documents	Strategy, Objectives and Policy Documents
ZFW R2: Functionality	Trace to R3	Author, Trace to R3	Author, Trace to R3, Govern	Author, Trace to R3, Govern, Measure, Budget	Author, Trace to R3, Govern, Measure, Budget, Forecast
ZFW R3: Resources to be Managed	Natural Language Business Rules	Natural Language and Formal Business Rules, Glossary	Natural Language and Formal Business Rules, Glossary	Natural Language and Formal Business Rules, Glossary	Natural Language and Formal Business Rules, Glossary
ZFW R3: Functionality	Access, Search and Report	Author, Access, search and Report, Test, Trace to R2 and R4	Author, Access, Search and Report, Test, Trace to R2 and R4, Govern	Author, Access, Search and Report, Trace to R2 and R4, Govern, Measure	Author, Access, Search and Report, Trace to R2 and R4, Govern, Measure, Predict
ZFW R4: Resources to be Managed		Designed Rule Set	Designed Rule Set	Designed Rule Set	Designed Rule Set
ZFW R4: Functionality		Trace to R3	Author and Trace to R3	Author, Test and Trace to R3	Author, Test, Measure and Trace to R3

Figure 5: Source Rule Repository – high level requirements matrix

This authoring environment, at its highest form of evolution, should provide the enterprise's leaders with the controls of the "guidance system" promised by the Business Rules Approach. It should properly integrate with the modeling tools used in the enterprise in data and process management, while at the same time be robust and complete in its Business Rules capabilities.

The Rule Design Environment

From the structured rule, and from the rule models contained in the authoring environment, the design environment is used to implement a system model constrained to the defined deployment environment. Here the rule is expressed in its technical expression, or the "technical rule." This can approximate code, or in the most evolved of rules engines, may bear a close resemblance to the structured rule. The design environment is by definition constrained by technology. A difficulty in the Business Rules Approach is that frequently the technology constraint is pre-existing. While this is not an unusual state in many systems development environments, it can be a particularly taxing problem for systems that conform to the Business Rules Approach.

The Rule Deployment Environment

These are actual instituted technical rules, in a form that may be consumed by rules engines and other execution environments. The importance of this environment turns on maintaining traceable links with accurate versioning from the source rules to the executable rules.

A Brief—But Important—Digression from Architecture

A few words are needed about some practical issues (for architects, this touches on dreaded issues of methodology) , even in this theoretical conversation about architecture. This digression is warranted by the frequency with which the high-risk situation described below is encountered, even in organizations with strong architecture groups.

This undesirable but common situation is where the technology constraints in the Design Environment are set by an organization's choice of a Business Rules Engine (BRE) or a BRMS.

There are two traps present in this situation.

The First Trap is that the architectural approach to business rule development is dictated by the development patterns practiced by the technology vendor.

"Best Practice" becomes "Vendor Practice," in which in most cases the rules authoring process is limited to the gathering of rules entered directly into the BRMS tool, and for only those rules best supported by that tool. Most vendors take pride in and differentiate their BRMS products by their development tools, many of which completely bypass best rules authoring practices that connect to the business audience to achieve rapid development cycles.

Notwithstanding vendor claims, insufficient business rules management is performed in these tools as they exist today. Typically the rules entered into the system are already highly formalized or are even analogous to direct code. The focus, in the past, of the BRMS vendors has been the pursuit of rapid development offered by the terse, declarative, atomic rule statement. While this advantage is real and significant, it has unfortunately led to the very rapid development of systems that once in service have hidden the business rules as fully—if not more completely—than traditional COBOL systems.

A good example is a recent decision by a *Fortune 100* company to replace a major—and successful—order processing system developed over many years on a BRMS platform with an expensive ERP system. The principal reason? "We don't know what the rules in the system are." The point here is that the mere use of a BRMS platform may provide technical agility, but there is no guarantee that its use will provide any more business agility than exists in a procedurally coded environment.

So the practice of only following vendor development patterns may unfortunately lead to the loss of some or all of the benefits of a Business Rules Approach, including, but not limited to:

- Loss of access by the business to the rules.

- Loss of traceability of the rules to their business objectives and sources.

- Inability to deploy the rules to other or multiple technologies.

The Second Trap occurs when the mandated BRMS is found to be poorly matched to the type of rules being used in a particular project or system. This leads to the nightmare scenario of failed projects, budget overruns, and unhappy customers. Many examples of this mismatch abound. Because there is frequently no separation of authoring environment from deployment, once the technology is deployed it is difficult, time-consuming and expensive to transform to another technology.

Similar, and even greater, difficulties occur where the business rules technology constraints are set by the requirement that the rules be executed by the rules engines embedded into a selected business process management tool. Here the difficulties are that in large part these tools have very limited function rule capability, and lack even the limited rules management facilities provided by the BRMS systems.

In contrast, best practice in the design environment is to set the technology constraints only when the types of rules, quantity of rules, and the appropriate use of rules and appropriate patterns of development are well-understood. Because of this, it is advisable to complete a scoping exercise (or even more preferably, a pilot exercise) in the authoring environment that provides a good sample of rules and a relatively complete rules model before defining and setting the desired technology constraints in the design environment.

Returning to the Architectural Considerations in the Design Environment

A wide range of patterns are available to architects in the design environment. BRMSs derive from two primary roots:

Knowledge engineering, which gave rise to expert systems. These have evolved over time and with advances such as the Rete algorithm into BRMSs that have advanced inference capabilities. These engines are ideally used in support of decisions where large quantities of rules are executed against relatively small amounts of data. Classically these are called "inference engines," whose strengths lie primarily in backward chaining algorithms. Their method of reaching a conclusion is to:

- Examine data to determine which rules reference that data.

- Test the conditions of the rules that reference this data to determine whether this requires additional pieces of data

- Determine which additional rules reference the additional data

- And so on until the chain is complete, at which point the engine is then responsible for determining the order in which the rules should correctly executed, and a conclusion is reached

The advantage of this approach is that the programmer is free to create declarative rules without considering in advance the sequence in which the rules may be used.

An example of this may be a group of rules defining customer status. When the customer name is submitted to the engine, and the engine has all available customer data and is requested to find the customer's status, it can be relied upon to gather from the stack of all rules the appropriate customer rules and resolve the customer status based upon the available customer data.

These engines are considered most appropriate for decision intensive systems, typified by insurance underwriting, credit assessment, and similar applications.

Process engineering, which evolved with the development of the Data Base engine, allows the separation of data from process and the definition of objects. Ultimately this led to the separation of rules from the code (as the code was in turn separated from data), and the development of BRMSs that are event-driven. In these engines an event (such as change in state of data) triggers the execution of rules. These engines are typically used for large quantities of data being processed against constraint and calculation rules, with relatively little inference being required. They are necessarily forward-chaining engines: they follow the chain of triggers of a sequence of rules until the chain is exhausted. These sequences (and their branches) have to be defined by the programmer, and the goal of the chain known in advance. They are very apt in transaction processing environments, where a series of constraints are applied to data as it is processed.

These rules tend to be focused on data constraints and transactions, leading to a 'fit' to applications that have intensive, large-scale business transactions at their core.

Which is the best engine ? While each type of engine can more or less perform the services of the other, there is no question that performance and function will be executed dramatically better by the appropriate engine:

"While it is possible to emulate an event-driven system using inference methods and vice versa, the key question of efficiency must be examined. In assessing the performance of BRMSs, the sensitivity to both the number of rules and the amount of data must be considered. Inference-driven engines scale well as the number of rules increases; however, performance of Rete-based engines degrades rapidly as data volume increases. Event-driven engines scale linearly, both with regard to the amount of data and with regard to the number of rules triggered by an event."[26]

As the business uses of rules engines evolves, developments are occurring that are beginning to blur the distinction between these engines. Traditional

---

26. Segal, Gil. "Business Rules for Business Transactions," Sapiens White Paper, 2005

architecture, while embedding a centralized set of transactional and data constraint rules in the data access tiers.

The concepts in Figure 6 can also be helpful when approaching problems such as rules embedded in commercial applications. These can be categorized in the same fashion, and thus referenced by tools or processes in the appropriate layers of the architecture.

A Special Problem: Business Rules versus Business Process Management

A particular issue that needs to be dealt with is the role of business rules vis-à-vis business process management. There abounds in many quarters the misguided notion that business rules are an encapsulated component of business process management. Too often, many enterprise architectures represent business rules within the larger container of the business process bubble. And then of course, there is the fact that many business process, workflow, and content management engines incorporate "business rules" that are programmable by the user. Since architecture is frequently driven by technology, the deployment of this technology leads to business rules being buried again, this time into the process engines.

All of this is unnecessary. The correct architectural approach can lead to an improvement in business process management implementations while maintaining a separation between process and business rules. Figure 4 shows a business rules model with a natural connection points between business rules in Column 6 and business process in Column 2. These points are, in the main:

- Business Process to Decision to Business Rule Set. It clearly shows the connecting point in Figure 4, while a more detailed illustration of the relationship is illustrated in Figure 7.
- Business Rule Glossary mapped to the Business Process Object Model, again shown in Figure 4.

By separating the components in the architecture at those points, the architecture enables business rules to be changed independently of process and vice versa. This preserves all the advantages of both business process and business rules management, significantly improving business agility.

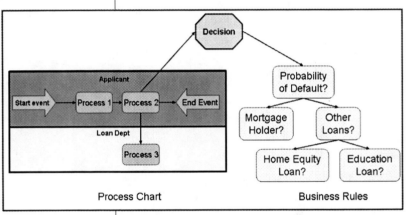

Figure 7:   Separating Business Rules From Process Using Decisions

Conclusion

For an enterprise that has made a commitment to pursue the Business Rules Approach, there is a significant reduction in risk and concomitant increase in reward to be had, by first defining needs using the KPI RMM™, and then building a business architecture to support those needs. The architecture should reflect the need to place the business firmly in control of business rules, and the greater the maturity that the enterprise needs to achieve, the greater the role of the business in managing the rules.

Part II
The Business Side of Business Rules

Aimed specifically at the business audience (but appropriate also for technical audiences), this section examines the crucial relationship of business rules to business processes and elevates the business policy maker to rule author. The four chapters cover the integration of business rules to a business engineering approach (Chapter 5), benefits achieved in combining business process modeling with business rules at a state government organization (Chapter 6), the dynamics of iterating process modeling and business rules (Chapter 7), and a major corporation's ground-breaking rule management software for its policy makers (Chapter 8).

Again, in their own words, below are quotes selected by each author to provide the reader with insights into each chapter:

"The business rules movement is catalyzing the desire of organizations to move towards a business engineering approach where the business specifications are no longer requirements that support the development of IT design. Rather, they are the business configuration that is expected to be loaded into the IT solution."

Chapter 5, Neal McWhorter

"Business users are directly involved in the business requirements identification and verification much earlier in the development process. The implementation of this tool [at Oregon Public Employee Retirement Systems] allowed us to consolidate business rule responsibilities from IT (QA) systems staff to the primary business users after appropriate training."

Chapter 6, Larry Ward and Jordan Masanga

"What is perhaps surprising is that the impact of business rules on these other model views and on their quality may be as significant as the achievement of clearly specified business rules. What proved most effective…was not a top-down, process-to-rules approach, but one that iterated between both perspectives."

Chapter 7, Art Moore and Michael Beck

"This chapter discusses our journey into more sophisticated and innovative software to empower the rule authors:

- A rule inquiry application to enable access to and inspection of rules

- A rule maintenance application to hide the idiosyncrasies of the rules engine (and allow for changing the rules engine)

- A rule analysis application to ensure integrity of new and changed rules

- A rule application emulator so rule authors can see the rules in action (simulated with data) prior to actual deployment in the target rules engine."

Chapter 8, John Semmel

5 Business Engineering and the Role of Business Rules

Neal McWhorter

A Definition of Business Engineering

The service industries, banking, insurance, and accounting, among others, have had a long-standing culture of separation between business work and work on tools to support the business. This separation came about naturally enough, since most of these industries existed in some form or the other prior to automation playing a significant role in their operations. But the technology as a tool approach is a business practice whose time has come and gone. Nowadays, technology is integrated into these businesses and what are being offered are technology-based services. Yet despite this huge change, most organizations have yet to address the internal divide within their organizations that separates business from technology. What is needed is an integrated approach that obliterates the old divide and brings the business back into direct control of the development of these technology-based products and services. We call this approach *business engineering.*

Business engineering is a holistic approach to business design that starts with the premise that automation solution design is *product design*. This is a big departure from most approaches that assume that automation solution design is engineering the supporting infrastructure to *operate the business*. What is it about the changes of the recent years that drives this shift in approach? *The fundamental shift in approach derives from a shift in ownership of knowledge.* Previously, people owned the knowledge, and they used tools to assist them. But since the tools were just an internal aid in performing the business, the knowledge that controlled a business's operations remained fundamentally in the hands of people. With the pervasive automation of businesses and the explosion of technology-based services as products in their own right, the balance has shifted. *Now the knowledge is embedded in the automation solution itself.* And because much of the business operates without any human judgments being made, there isn't any going back.

The remainder of this chapter covers:

- Three ways to represent knowledge behind business engineering

- The importance of capturing decisions in business engineering

- Business decisioning

- Incorporating business level specifications with automation specifications

- The gap in business entities today

- The gap in business processes today

- The Business Rule Revolution

- Back to business decisions

- Summary

Three Ways to Represent Knowledge Behind Business Engineering

The knowledge that we are engineering to support our business is represented in one of three ways: as business entities, business processes, or business rules. There is no simple explanation for where to draw the boundary among these three ways of capturing business knowledge. Each involves a trade-off between comprehensibility and ease of change. Business entities represent business knowledge that we believe is relatively fixed. We also believe that by making the concepts fixed we lose little in flexibility and reduce the complexity of the problem when they are represented as entities. Business processes define the possible paths along which business work can be performed, as well as the actual business work itself. The type of structured approach used in business process analysis produces specifications that make the possible paths readily understandable while obscuring the policies that drive those choices. In the cases of business entities and business processes, changes to either are much more visible than would be a rule-driven description of the same change, because the rules implied within each are implicit within these patterns.

Adding business rules to the mix has a dramatic impact on those practices. It allows the added ability to formalize the more fluid business judgments that are central to business agility. To understand the full extent of this impact, it's important to understand the limitations of current techniques.

The Importance of Capturing Decisions in Business Engineering

As it's practiced today, most business engineering begins with and remains focused on business process analysis. The emphasis on business processes is driven by a focus on metrics that capture the operational characteristics of the process through measures such as: cost per unit of work performed, process execution time, and defect rates. There is nothing wrong with these metrics per se, but the operational excellence they focus on isn't the whole story. What's missing is an approach to systematically examine and manage all the decisions that underlie a process's execution and to control the rates of flows through the various paths defined by the business processes. You can think of these decisions as the valves and gates in a factory that control the work flowing down each path and at which rates. More simply we can say that business rules implement the decisions that support the *business policies* which guide the business work under specified circumstances.

In most current approaches to capturing business rules, the rules are relegated to details captured about decision points within a business process. For example, in a fulfillment process we might capture a decision point that determines that all the items in an order must be in inventory before any items are pulled for an order. But if we stop for a moment and examine this decision, we can see that what we are really asking for is a decision about the order which, if it is made, will allow the fulfillment process to continue down the path that leads to pulling items ordered from inventory. That is, there is a decision in the business process about orders that examines a judgment about the order and which has its own (implied) definition and existence and which is then called into play at appropriate points in relevant processes. That judgment is an important piece of our business engineering that is seldom explicitly acknowledged.

The lack of formalization of business judgments means that when a business domain expert goes to examine how a policy was engineered into the business, it is difficult to tell where to begin. After all, policies often apply across many business processes. So how would one locate all the business processes where the policy is implemented?

Capturing and managing business judgments is the area that exposes the greatest weaknesses in our current approach to business engineering and delivers perhaps the greatest opportunity for business improvement. Most approaches simply fail to acknowledge a formal way of capturing business judgments and relating them to business processes, business entities, business metrics, and eventually to underlying business policies and rules. How can this be? Process analysis is typically focused on conceptual design of processes rather than operational design. That means that organizations do not expect that their business process specifications are in fact the exact specifications that are being executed. This type of approach works tolerably well if the focus of the exercise is on engineering the individual activities being done within the business process to minimize the number of them, arrange their order to minimize bottlenecks, reduce the cost of executing them, and support monitoring them for quality. Basically, if the intent is to engineer a solution that is effective in handling the high-volume-straight-through-processing type of interactions, then this type of approach to business engineering can be very effective. However, if the intent is to deal with the much smaller percentage of cases that follow some kind of exception path, then this type of approach is woefully inadequate.

But in the current business environment, where visibility into the internals of an organization's processes is a key competitive advantage, can we afford to only engineer for the normal cases? After all, the exception paths are the paths that allow an organization to adapt to customers' needs and that deserve special business attention. Even more important, exception paths provide opportunities to interact with customers in a situation where they can have an unexpected positive experience—a situation which is the key to achieving customer loyalty. Something is missing from our traditional business process analysis approaches, that prevents our business analysis from being able to handle these exception paths and thereby become the real operational definition of how these business processes behave. Once again, the answer is business rules or more properly business decisioning.

Business Decisioning

Business decisioning is the discipline of taking business information and applying particular tactics to it, so that new information is produced that embodies some kind of human judgment. There are a variety of ways of doing this, including mathematical approaches such as optimization and constraint solving for dealing with situations calling for finding a "best solution," as well as fuzzy logic and other kinds of probabilistic reasoning focusing on finding the most likely solution. But most business reasoning is of a simpler kind, which involves reaching a conclusion, even if the decision is not so straight-forward. This is the kind of reasoning that is the focus of the business rules movement. The recognition of this is what is behind the recent emergence of business rules as a distinct aspect of business engineering in its own right.

The emergence of decisioning and business rules as a formalism, then, is a natural business maturity progression. That is, once the business defines and manages the "normal paths" through critical business processes, the next evolutionary step is to seek to leverage the exception paths for business advantage.

Incorporating Business Level Specifications with Automation Specifications

We talked at the beginning about the importance of organizations seeing automation solution design as an integral part of product design. To achieve this, we have to be able to incorporate a business level specification within the automation specifications. In particular, this means we need to stop creating business process and business entity models that have no corresponding element in the delivered automation solution. While other industries have struggled with this problem, many of them have a physical metaphor which they can reproduce in their automation solutions to act as this bridge. This allows business domain experts to continue to write specifications in terms of those physical elements, even though they may no longer exist.

In the service industries, things are a little bit different because existing business work and existing business specifications have seldom been explicitly formulated into an executable framework. Domain experts don't have a physical metaphor to use as the *de facto* way of structuring how their business needs are expressed in the automation solution. That means that we have to construct a metaphor for our business experts, as well as adapt it for direct use to configure the operation of our automation solutions. Because we can't expect to succeed by creating a completely foreign metaphor, we are compelled to take existing concepts that these business experts are familiar with and weave them into a coherent executable framework. This framework needs to be able to represent a specification that could be executed as it is documented, but which also could be mapped onto a more sophisticated implementation. We can think of this last step as designing a factory to efficiently produce our product.

To understand this, let's take a traffic light system as an example. Originally these systems were complex to configure. Traffic lights had physical switches in them that controlled the sequencing of lights and the intervals between them. Timers were used to determine when to send a signal to a light to initiate the transition to a stop or go state. Gradually the physical location and even existence of these elements became less and less relevant, because complex traffic management systems created abstractions for these components in software. But for the individuals configuring these systems, the established concepts of switches and timers were how they still conceptualized what they were doing. Because of this, traffic management systems today provide concepts that are familiar to those experts who configure these systems. By making it possible to configure these systems using a specification written in the domain experts' own terms, these systems have made it possible for completely new traffic management solutions to be designed entirely by the traffic management experts. In addition, the new automated traffic management systems made it possible for the traffic management experts to design much more complex systems that they could within the limitations of the old physical component systems.

In the area of business engineering, there are also existing concepts that are part of the vernacular of business engineering. We can adopt these into our vocabulary of concepts to form the basis for how business domain experts can go about specifying business solutions. These concepts include: business processes, business entities, business rules, and business events. But tying these together into an executable specification requires relating them in a way that is not carried out by most practitioners today.

At first blush, it seems that current practices for defining concepts and their relationships is an area that is already in line with our needs. Existing modeling techniques for enterprise conceptual data modeling and for enterprise business entity models provide a defined way for us to identify concepts, the relationships among them, and characteristics of those concepts. However, traditional business analytic techniques don't begin with the premise that a set of business-defined concepts will become the basis for defining the executing business logic of an automatable specification. This means that today's business analytic techniques fail to recognize that the IT implementation of knowledge is essential to a business understanding of the knowledge. But, ironically, the IT implementation of that knowledge is exactly the implementation that the business is truly running with. While the IT implementation is polluted with technical considerations that the business does not want or need to be exposed to, the lack of a clear separation between *IT engineering concepts* and *business concepts* means that we don't have an abstraction available that represents the real knowledge model the business operates against with the implementation details removed. It is this separation of business and engineering concepts that John Zachman addresses in his Framework of Enterprise Information Architecture (See Chapter 3 from John Zachman for insights into the Zachman Framework).

The Gap in Business Entities Today

Consider the customer entity. Organizations usually have multiple systems in which the concept of a customer is represented. These systems range from CRM and ERP systems to in-house product support systems. What do we do when we have multiple customer concepts across these systems? Typically, we have one of two choices: abstract a single concept of customer for business specification purposes, or deal with them as unique concepts, unrelated to each other. What we don't typically do is create a series of abstract concepts that support the way the business actually uses the multiple customer concepts. Let's say that we have what we believe is the same customer, in both an ERP solution and an in-house marketing system. In fact, we might find that 99% of the customer instances are virtually identical. Are these two different systems supporting a single concept? If so, this is a technical issue, not a business issue. But what if the reason that some of the marketing entries are different is because the marketing department has found that for some specific customers, using certain internal organizational names is a much more effective way of getting material routed to the right people. At this point, we've identified two related but different concepts. By leaving this gap, we build a shaky foundation on top of which to build our business engineering specification.

The Gap in Business Processes Today

Our current practices for defining business processes also have similar problems. In fact, some of the problems in this area are a direct result of the issues we have just discussed in the business entity engineering area. After all, business process definitions exist primarily to show the paths along which business work can be performed. The business work that is being performed on these paths is manipulation of business entities. So if our existing business entity model is not an accurate representation of the entities that we have available to work on, then it becomes impossible for us to accurately define the work. But additional issues exist that are particular to the business process analysis area itself. In particular, business processes are frequently modeled as large monolithic definitions that, when compared to how work is actually done within an organization, turn out to be only approximations of what is really happening. This gap means that the definitions being developed aren't really specifications that could be used to actually configure the process definitions that an organization is run by.

In the case of business processes, the reason for this gap is a bit more complex. One of the primary areas where business process definitions diverge from reality is when dealing with exceptions; in this case, exceptional flows. While it's easy to think conceptually of processes as being a set of sequential actions that follow defined branches based upon control points, this is typically a simplification of what really happens within organizations. The key fallacy is that the way that an activity within a process triggers the activity that follows it is no more complex than the completion of that first activity. This is particularly true when the activities that we're talking about involve some kind of human intervention. For example, let's say we document an approval process as having a "Submit Request" activity followed by a "Determine Disposition" activity. Let's assume that the "Determine Disposition" activity involves a person examining the submitted request and making a judgment about whether or not to approve it. Does the person making this judgment actually start doing this as soon as the request is submitted? Obviously, this wouldn't be an accurate representation of how things really happen.

Alternatively, we could claim that "Determine Disposition" is really an abstraction for a work queue. But this approach is also problematic. If we treat this activity as a work queue, then we need to define a related process that describes how approval is granted. We don't want to include this process in our general business process because we are really agnostic about how this happens. And, in fact, it's quite possible that there are multiple approval processes that exist (e.g. supervisor and operations level approval processes), any one of which is sufficient to generate the approval within a core process we might call "Handle Requests." This is in fact a very typical process pattern made use of by organizations. What we are seeing here is an example of a family of interrelated processes. Each of these processes triggers something in the other process, but they aren't part of each other. For example, the supervisor approval process might both allow the "Handle Request" process to proceed and cause the process for getting operational approval to withdraw the work from that role's work queue, since the supervisor has already approved it.

Beyond these oversimplifications of process flows, there is another major limitation to current business process analysis techniques. This other limitation involves the process- centric nature of this kind of work. While process-centric analysis is a powerful technique for bringing together all the interested parties and making sure they align to the same goals, it does obscure the role of business policy. Take, for example, the decision that all purchases over $1,000 must be pre-approved by a supervisor-level position. Because there are many different business processes that support creating a purchase request, it would be very difficult to change this policy and have assurance that the revised policy would be applied to all relevant processes. That's because, without a Business Rules Approach, there is no traceability from the policy to its implementation across the business enterprise. In a purely process-centric point of view, there isn't the concept of a judgment which has an existence independent of any particular process. So when we go to change what appears to be a single policy, we instead have to locate and modify a series of control points within any number of business processes.

The Business Rule Revolution

The weaknesses that we've identified in both business entity and business process specification are issues that have existed for some time. This has been possible because there has not been a strong movement towards an integrated business engineering approach that provides a metaphor for business experts and that can also be used to configure the automated solution. This is where the Business Rule Revolution comes into play.

The Business Rule Revolution is driven by forces relevant to both business entity and business process analysis. However, the focus from the business rules side is not only on the conceptual understanding of the business specification. Rather, business rules are being driven by the realization of organizations that one of the major impediments to change is that their business domain experts can't directly control the business operations by managing and evolving its policies and rules appropriately. In other words, the business rules movement is catalyzing the desire of organizations to move towards a business engineering approach where the business specifications are no longer requirements that support the development of IT design. Rather, they are the business configuration that is expected to be loaded into the IT solution. Business rules' interdependency with both business entities and business processes means that, for rules to be directly maintained by business domain experts, the entire supporting foundation upon which they are built or with which they interact must also be executionally complete.

One of the key ways in which business rules cause a business specification to be an executionally complete specification is via their interaction with business entities and business processes. Business rules need a vocabulary to allow the creators of those rules to express the rules in both a language that is natural to them as well as one that has rigorous semantics. That means that the vocabulary for rules is derived from the business entity model, business rule glossary model, or fact model. This vocabulary can also be derived from the business rules themselves, because business rules define new pieces of knowledge that are beyond what is captured by business entity models. It doesn't take much of a leap to see that if business rules are maintained directly by business domain experts, and that business rules are to be directly executable, then the new kind of business model (comprised of business processes, business rules, and a model of business terms) must itself be an accurate representation of the available business concepts.

Business rules play a major role in helping drive business process specifications toward a level of formality that can produce executionally complete specifications. A business rules approach can also help address another weakness of most business process specifications, the role of business events. Business events have a number of different sources. External sources are common and are standardized in some industries through standards such as ACORD and SWIFT. But not all events are standardized. Some events are specific to an organization's design of their internal processes and are direct outcomes of these business process designs. We saw an example of this in our earlier discussion of the "Handle Request" process and how it was related to the "Operational Approval" and "Supervisory Approval" process via business events. Yet another way that business events can be generated is using business rules.

Business rules can be used to define that a business situation has occurred. A common example is the use of a business rule to detect that a business policy has been violated. For example, let's say that an organization has a policy that all orders over $1,000,000 should be assigned to a dedicated sales agent. This is something that might be done as part of taking the order, but if this process involves a manual decision about staffing, it may not always be able to be done automatically. If we define a rule that captures this condition, we can detect that the situation "Large Order Placed without Assigned Sales Agent" has occurred. We can indicate to business processes that this has occurred by making it a business event. By making it a business event we decouple the business processes from these policy enforcement opportunities. This happens because the rules don't need to know who cares about the event. The rules simply determine the conditions under which a specific situation of business interest occurs. On the business process side, the "Assign Dedicated Sales Agent" process doesn't know the rules that determine why the event occurs. The process simply knows that appropriate conditions were concluded to be true, hence, the appropriate process should be initiated.

But it's also possible that we have other processes that potentially are interested in this event, such as a marketing process (because customers placing an initial large order are potentially growth customers) or a "Sales Force Allocation" process (needing to respond to the more general need to revaluate the allocation of individuals to accounts). By separating out the detection of the situation into rules that determine an event, we allow changes to business processes to occur much more rapidly, because the events are business specification elements whose definition is not specific to any particular business process.

Back to Business Decisions

Business rules have an even more central role to play in creating more rigorous, but agile, business engineering specifications. That role is in defining how business judgments support the creation of decisions. These judgments are the missing element of most business engineering efforts. Very much like business events, business judgments have a separate existence apart from the context of any particular business process. In fact, much of the vocabulary that we use when we discuss business engineering is centered on these business judgments. For example, we talk about orders being approved for a premium customer if their account is in good standing. In this case, someone being a premium customer and having an account in good standing may be considered two business judgments, each of which is determined by its own set of underlying detailed business rules. Why are they business judgments? Because these are stand-alone business concepts that are directly manipulated by business domain experts. This makes them essential to become part of the metaphor we are building for these experts to manipulate. In addition, by giving this business judgment existence independent of any particular business process we allow for the possibility that there may be many processes that care about whether a customer has an account in good standing. Typical examples would be processes in marketing, sales, and billing. By identifying these processes as all using the same business judgment, we enable the business to make policy-related changes to these business judgments without impacting the business processes. After all, the business processes don't really need to know why an account is in good standing. All they care about is that the appropriate decision controls the paths chosen in a process. So if a business decides to change the policies in a way that doesn't change the business work being done then all that needs to be done is to change the rules that support this business judgment, and all processes that refer to this judgment will immediately reflect this change. For example, if the company wants to increase the percentage of orders automatically approved for premium customers in good standing, tweaking of the rules that underly the approval judgement will be all that is required.

This idea of identifying business judgments has a much broader impact than it initially appears. After all, traditionally business judgments have been examined in the past strictly in terms of how they control business processes and therefore they usually don't have a high degree of reuse across multiple business processes. But business judgments typically aren't monolithic. Most business judgments are built upon a series of intermediate business judgments. So in our previous example, it is quite possible that our judgments that a customer is a premium customer is built out of a set of intermediate judgments such as: the customer has a valid volume purchase contract in place, the customer bought more than $500,000 in goods or services in the past year, or because a manager has directly authorized that the customer will get premium customer benefits. Any one of these could be sufficient to support the higher level business judgment that a customer is a premium customer. However, these same intermediate judgments may be used to build up other top-level business judgments that business processes will examine. For example, the judgment that a customer has a valid volume purchasing contract in place could play a role in billing because this volume purchasing agreement may require a yearly contract renewal to be maintained, as well as a period credit evaluation. These higher-level decisions probably aren't of interest to the sales process though even though they probably are to the account management processes.

In fact what we typically find is that most business specifications contain a lot of information about business judgments, without a formal way of fitting the judgments into the business specification process. By capturing the business judgments as legitimate elements of the business specification and using business rules to round out the judgments, we get a highly integrated business specification. The business processes now have the judgments and events available to them that they need to control their flow, because pure business processes are about sequence, not about decisioning logic. The rules underlying the business judgments make use of the vocabulary derived from the entity model (or rule-related vocabulary model). And the business events and business judgments themselves expand the vocabulary to allow the business to refer to these derived concepts in a structured way that isolates the impact of changes to reflect natural business boundaries. This last idea is possibly the most important. *By making business decisions and events correspond to real-world business concepts, the impact of making changes to the business specification should correspond to the business domain experts' own expectations of the impact, because the concepts directly correspond to their own way of thinking about the problem.*

Summary

The integrated business specification approach outlined here runs counter to many existing organizational boundaries in several ways.

1. It focuses on empowering business experts to be able to create new business products directly in many cases, without requiring much involvement of IT engineering. The approach does this by

shifting the paradigm from one where the business develops requirements to be translated into operational specifications into one where IT engineering delivers a framework that presents the business concepts, decisions, and supporting rule pieces (conditions and conclusions) as real elements that a business specification can work with.

2. Direct support for business concepts within the implementation framework allows a business specification to become a configuration that is loaded into the solution. This gives the business direct control of the operational behavior of the solution.

3. To achieve this, the business specifications must be executionally complete. And in order to achieve that, we need more rigor in the way we perform business entity and business process specification and integration with the Business Rules Approach.

4. None of this is to diminish the role of IT engineering. A business engineering approach allows IT resources to focus on IT engineering rather than on business specification translation. Giving business direct control over the operational specifications is a paradigm shift that ·is the most promising path to increasing the rate of innovation in a market that increasingly is innovation driven.

6 A BPM-Driven Approach to Business Rules

Larry Ward and Jordan Masanga

About OPERS

The Oregon Public Employee Retirement System (OPERS) began its arduous but never-ending trip using the Business Rules Approach in 1999 under a large IT-driven reengineering project. With minimum in-house business rules knowledge, but an absolute directive, we jumped on the wagon—and it seemed as if it was bouncing and careening through the ruts being carved in the Oregon Trail.

OPERS's first steps were to identify staff roles and create a business rules development infrastructure, in which business rules were identified and organized for development within systems. With insufficient budget and time, we had to base business rule development on a low-technology/low-cost approach.

During the next three years, for every three steps forward, we seemed to take two steps backward. Due to pressures of a highly visible reengineering project, an active state legislature, and critical court decisions, OPERS executives were unable to dedicate consistent support to the development of business rules. The resulting "priority of the week" directly impacted staff ability to develop business rules in the optimum manner and timeframe. Fortunately, OPERS had a small, but determined, business rules team that recognized both the importance of, and need for, a single repository for authoring and managing business rules and a business process management plan. The remainder of this chapter covers:

- Background

- Business drivers for OPERS's business rules

- Establishing a business rules group and related tools

- IT-driven approach versus business and BPM-driven approach

- The business-driven project

- Summary

Background

OPERS provides state, local, and higher education agencies with multiple pension, deferred compensation, and retiree health insurance programs. The original plan is a defined benefit plan; the new plan includes both a defined benefit plan and a defined contribution plan. Additionally, we administer a deferred compensation plan, retiree health insurance, and long-term care insurance.

Business Drivers for OPERS's Business Rules

There are many business drivers for OPERS to justify using the Business Rules Approach. These drivers include regulatory requirements, litigation concerns, audit concerns, and the need for changes in rules.

Let's start with federal and state statutes, regulations, administrative rules, and case law from court rulings. The primary business driver is the statutory requirement that the OPERS retirement plans continue to meet IRS requirements to be qualified plans, while a secondary driver is customer support to the members, retirees, and employers who participate in OPERS plans.

Most OPERS business drivers are related to our retirement plans' being contained in and based upon state statutes, with detailed administrative rules that correspond to the statutes. The Oregon Legislature is in session every other two years for a nine-month session. Historically, OPERS is affected by new legislation that occurs during these sessions. These changes impact business rules and processes that may or may not have been fully implemented before the latest legislative session starts or ends.

Litigation is another major business driver. Court rulings for the last fifteen years have driven major changes to how OPERS plans were administered, and in 2003 they drove the legislative creation of an adjunct second plan. Court rulings always create changes to business rules and processes—some retroactively.

Audits are a business driver. OPERS activities are routinely audited by external state regulatory agencies and functions. Audit findings have the potential to change business practices, business requirements, and business rules and to impact current and planned IT projects.

Changes occur rapidly at OPERS and have cascading impact on the enterprise. Agility is key to responding to ever-changing business demands, necessitating business-driven projects with centralized management of business and system requirements. Therefore, taking control of requirements, including business rules, stakeholder needs, use cases, requirement specifications, and operational processes and procedures was our first priority. However, due to budgetary constraints, a commercial business rules engine was not an option. Instead, OPERS extended existing use of the IBM Rational RequisitePro® requirements and use case management tool to develop separate databases within a single repository. As a result, traceability between multiple requirement types allows OPERS to manage business change with greater agility and quality.

Establishing a Business Rules Group and Related Tools

The OPERS Quality Assurance Manager is organizationally aligned under the Information Systems Division and has the role of technology development and quality assurance (QA). The responsibility for developing business rules was originally coordinated by QA (1999—2004), but was realigned to a business unit in 2005. The Business Process Management (BPM) methodology is currently championed by QA, but will also evolve to a business unit responsible for processes.

The Rational Unified Process (RUP) methodology has been the basis for our IT projects since 1998. The RUP methodology has four phases: Inception, Elaboration, Construction, and Transition. Using RUP, OPERS applies incremental development between the phases. IBM Rational RequisitePro® is the IT tool set the agency has available for development projects. We selected it as the database and repository for business rule requirements.

Senior staff changes, cancellation of the reengineering project, and the resulting scramble to keep using the processes and tools started in the cancelled reengineering project eventually led us to research the Business Process Management (BPM) approach/methodology. Determining how OPERS could implement this shift/change in development methods and business organizational approach became a major question and discussion.

Key QA staff read Howard Smith and Peter Fingar's *Business Process Management (BPM): The Third Wave* and Andrew Spanyi's *Business Process Management is a Team Sport: Play it to Win*!, then brainstormed ways to use this approach and methodology, initially for IT projects and eventually for other activities and workload within the agency.

Legislative approval of a major systems conversion project for OPERS in 2004 provided a vehicle that let us begin the change process from IT-driven to business-driven projects and contracts. This major conversion project is an addition to a project that is implementing a legislatively dictated new retirement plan that is adjunct to, but not totally separate from, the existing retirement plan. The system architecture for the new program uses a new server-based tool set.

IT-Driven Approach versus Business and BPM-Driven Approach

A small team of business and IT managers applied lessons learned in the previous project to the contract requirements for the conversion project. The contract requirements identified the use of a Business Process Management (BPM) development methodology. The initial project implementing a new plan structure required renewed executive sponsorship of business rules, which re-energized our critical business rule development process. Both projects required business rules to be available early in the development process and traceable to the various business and development requirements. Moving business rule development and maintenance to the first RUP phase of Inception allowed increased quality, mitigation of risks, and accurate results when the system developers started doing their development work during the RUP Elaboration and Construction phases. Another benefit would be the likelihood that the project schedule could be maintained, due to a reduced quantity of rework resulting from inaccurate or unidentified requirements.

We have found that the classic IT-driven approach is applied to individual IT projects. It evolves from technical staff guiding a process of fact-finding from meetings and notes, and proceeds to requirement and business rule development in the later stages of RUP Elaboration and Construction Phases. Business rules and information captured in one project may or may not be shared or integrated with other or future projects.

The business and BPM-driven approach we use leverages industry best-practice standards. This method strongly supports structured approaches in business rules, requirements, design, implementation, and testing.

Figure 8 illustrates our view and comparison of the development approaches from a business user and developer viewpoint.

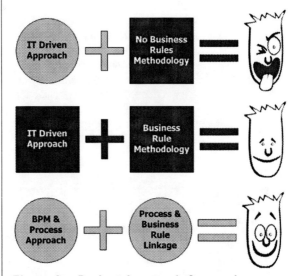

Figure 8: Project Approach Comparisons

Remember the bouncing and careening through the ruts worn in the Oregon Trail and the "priority of the week" issues? Well, the wagons are still sporting the unsprung axels and no springs for the seats! However, in applying BPM-driven methodology, we have been working hard to design a system of shock absorbers, springs, and a wagon more suited to the travelers' (business users) needs than what the builders (IT developers) thought was needed for the wagon.

Lean and agile BPM is having positive effects on the latest OPERS system conversion project. Business users are directly involved in the business requirements identification and verification much earlier in the development process. The end goals are to increase business and systems agility and create technical solutions to support business processes. Examples are: business process models; business rules; business process metrics; business procedures; stakeholder needs; supplemental specifications; use cases, use case specifications, and use case models. Figure 9 compares the differences in gathering requirements between a typical IT-driven approach project and a business and BPM-driven project.

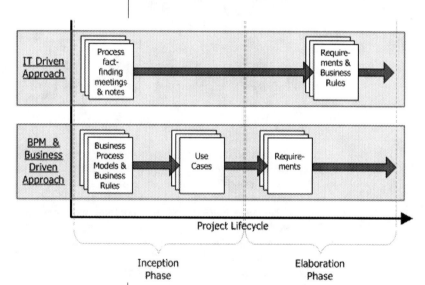

Figure 9: Project Approach Changes in Requirements Gathering

When we analyzed and compared the two approaches, it became evident that there are several distinct key differences. Figure 10 identifies these key differences as an overlay to the Figure 9 comparison of the two approaches.

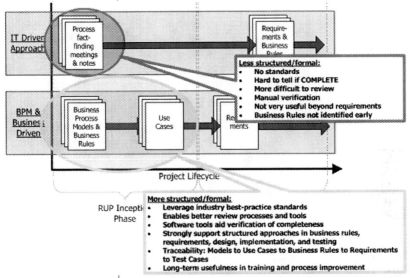

Figure 10: Process Approach Structure Comparison

Our analysis found the IT-driven fact-finding methodology is based on a less structured, less formal development approach. Generally, there are few standards used in discovering business expectations. Analysis of business and QA experiences revealed that it can be hard to tell when IT-driven projects are really complete. The processes of and artifacts resulting from development activity are difficult for business users or QA to review or verify, because there tend to be no clearly defined requirements or measurement points. Business rules and requirements are typically developed later in the IT-driven approach.

Analysis of the business and BPM-driven methodology convinced us that it is the model to use. It is based on a more structured/formal approach that leverages industry best-practice standards, to enable better review processes and tools for business users and QA. The software tools available for BPM aid verification and completeness. BPM strongly supports structured approaches in business rules, requirements, design, implementation, and testing. The tools also provide traceability, linkage of models, use cases, business rules, requirements, and test cases. BPM methodology also provides long-term usefulness in training, process improvement, and risk management.

Figure 11 illustrates the difference in workload distribution of business involvement between the two project approaches by overlaying the IT-driven approach with the business and BPM-driven approach.

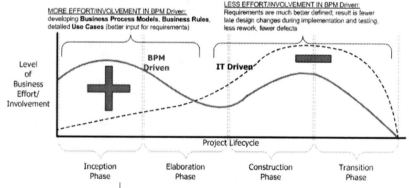

Figure 11: Project Approach Comparison

In Figure 11, the IT-driven approach resembles a whale. It shows that critically important business user involvement occurs much later in the project and usually poses a much greater risk to the project than the business and BPM-driven approach, due to poorly defined requirements and business rules. Design changes in the later stages/phases tend to affect testing activities and the project schedule, and to be more costly than those in earlier stages/phases.

The business and BPM-driven approach resembles a two-hump camel. Figure 11 depicts much earlier business user involvement in a project. As a result, requirements are much better defined and there are fewer late design changes during testing and implementation, less rework, and fewer defects. Early business involvement also allows for developing more accurate business process models, business rules, and detailed use cases that create better requirements input. Early involvement of system testers with this process and the business users allows for more accurate testing results.

Our business processes have changed due to this migration from IT-driven to BPM-driven development methods. Figure 12 identifies the major differences.

Old Method	Process Driven
• IT Driven	• Business Driven
• Modeling for system implementation	• Modeling for process improvement
• Few metrics designed into system	• Metrics built-into system design
• Stakeholder needs captured but not traced	• Stakeholder needs captured and traced
• System & Organization in functional silos	• Processes modeled across functions in end-to-end process across organization
• Manual BR database update	• Automated BR database update

Figure 12: Business Process Changes

The Business-Driven Project

Our Business Rules Project began in 1999. The business-driven project began in early 2005. We were constrained to use our existing software tools. Our objectives in using Rational RequisitePro® were to develop process, business rule, and requirement database repositories, and to associate those databases (traceability) to maintain versioned business rule and process information. Business rules are captured in RequisitePro, while the Microsoft Word documents are maintained and versioned in a Rational ClearCase® repository. RequisitePro is also used to capture elements, stakeholder needs, use cases, and requirements. Figure 13 shows the resulting matrix of traceabilities between the different databases.

Requirement Type	Features	Use Cases	Supplementary Spec	Business Rules Spec	User Interface Spec	Business Rules	Business Procedures
Stakeholder Needs	X						
Features		X	X				
Use Cases	X			X	X		X
Supplementary Spec	X						
Business Rule Spec		X				X	
User Interface Spec		X					
Business Rules				X			
Business Procedures		X					

Figure 13: RequisitePro® Requirement Type Traceability Matrix

The on-going and evolving Business Rules Project has faced many issues: management challenges, database maintenance process, knowledge of tool capabilities, business rule availability to end-users, too much work and too little time, and both major and minor development projects requiring accurate and rapid development of rules. Through all of these, we gained the necessary expertise, and both the business rule process and QA acceptance test process have been continually improved. Figure 14 depicts our current RequisitePro® databases.

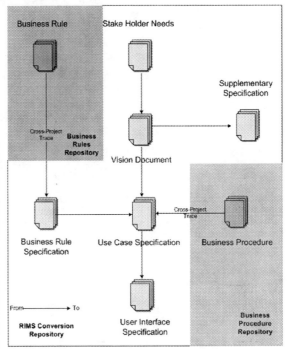

Figure 14: RequisitePro® Database Repositories Diagram

The manual maintenance of the business rule portion of the databases and repositories was very labor-intensive. OPERS had to find a more viable maintenance process and align process responsibilities to automate the database maintenance process. This resulted in a project we titled RequisitePro® Database Repository Maintenance Process Improvement. To achieve the process improvement goal, we developed a front-end program and process that automated the manual updates to multiple business rules database repositories, named Business Rules Transaction Application (BRTA). The BRTA tool incorporates a business rule process workflow from identification through approval and QA reviews to automated updates to the appropriate repositories. The final piece of the workflow makes the current approved version of business rules available for use by business users.

The implementation of this tool allowed us to consolidate business rule responsibilities from IT (QA) systems staff to the primary business users after appropriate training. The primary user is our Business Rules Writing Team. QA is a secondary user. The BRTA tool allows independent QA reviews of business rules. This process and tool ensures multiple databases and repositories agree at any point in time. Figure 15 shows the success of this process improvement project.

Activity	Manual Process	Automated Process
QA Business Rule Documents	3 to 20 hours weekly	1 to 2 hours weekly
Copy Data into Requisite Pro®	5 to 20 hours weekly	0
Copy Business Rule Word Documents to ClearCase®	3 to 10 hours weekly	0
Update Business Rules site on Intranet	10 to 30 weekly	0
Approved Rules Available to Users	2 to 3 weeks	3 to 5 days
Databases Concurrent & Accurate	Low to Medium	High

Figure 15: RequisitePro® Database Repository Maintenance Process Improvements

Summary

Development of business rules and the repository affected how OPERS develops and maintains software. Application of BPM has allowed us to implement a business-driven project process. OPERS projects are now centered on early development of: business process models; inputs/outputs, steps, and workflows; stakeholder needs; requirements; and identifying roles and responsibilities. Developing business rules that support business process models has been shifted to the earliest stage/phase of a project. We can now create a business and system requirements traceability matrix. This allows OPERS to drive requirements through implementation and change management. The QA and User Acceptance test plans and testing results are more accurate and responsive to any late changes due to an early identification of requirements and business rules.

What did we learn about business rules and BPM as we traveled along this bumpy and very heavily-rutted road?

- A dedicated team of business users with experience and industry knowledge is essential.

- Unwavering executive support is absolutely necessary.

- A Business Rules Engine (BRE) would have made much of the effort more efficient.

- A BRE would allow simulation of proposed changes to better identify issues and risks.

- Business users and IT staff need a business rules repository.

- Business cases must be planned and developed for the toolsets required.

- Contractors should be required to use BRE for all systems development.

- BPM and associated toolsets is a very good methodology to use in today's marketplace

7

Modeling the Business: Improving Process Models through Business Rules

Art Moore and Michael Beck

Introduction

Business rules, as a distinct focus of interest in the business systems model, had humble beginnings. In the 1980's business rules became a subject of discussion in the data management community. To many at that time and in that context, the phrase "business rules" simply meant the referential integrity rules to be applied to data. It soon expanded to the broader context of rules about what were valid states of data, such as "All preferred customers must have an account balance of at least $100,000." In fact, today some rule software takes this "data-centric" approach to defining and managing rules.

As these technologies have matured along with those originating out of artificial intelligence roots, and as the demand for system agility has continued to grow, business rules have begun to assume a more prominent role in business systems architecture and systems development. The basic idea is that business rules should be specified and implemented so as to make them readily accessible and independently changeable as needed, in a context that is as business-friendly as possible. Interesting issues of governance, consistency and traceability start to surface when embarking on this path, but the fundamental concept is a compelling one.

In conceiving and designing business systems, then, when do you begin to think about business rules? How exactly do they integrate with the other component parts of a business system specification? Fairly neat and satisfying arguments have been made for independent treatment of business rules throughout the systems life cycle, from early visioning through development. While drawing on such theory, we have, through research and a series of projects over the last several years, sought to identify what works in actual practice. These projects looked at real world business problems while also examining how best to integrate business rules specification into the system life cycle. A major objective was to improve the clarity and completeness of delivered business specifications through formal treatment of business rules, but to do so as efficiently as possible, without adding prohibitive cost and time.

Not surprisingly, our experience shows that being successful at separating and managing business rules requires that we understand them in context. Business rule specification does not happen in isolation but as part of a complete business model, integrated with the other business system views such as process, data, organization and location. What *is* perhaps surprising is that the impact of business rules on these other model views and on their quality may be as significant as the achievement of clearly specified business rules. The subject of this chapter is how business rules are found to integrate with the rest of the business model, particularly process, data, testing and requirements statements, and the impact on these areas. Therefore, this chapter covers:

- The impact of business rules on the process model

- The impact of business rules on the data model

- Business rules and business system requirements

- Business rules and testing

- Summary

The Impact of Business Rules on the Process Model

Possibly the most common perspective today among systems practitioners is that attention to rules comes at the end of business analysis, while moving into design and development. This viewpoint more or less reflects traditional practice. Business analysts are most familiar with process modeling of one form or another. For them, and for many business stakeholders as well, this is the most natural way to visualize and communicate about what the business "is." Thus business rules are viewed as simply an adjunct or further detailing of process specifications. As it turns out, this approach is more likely to carry forward arbitrary procedural components of both the current business process and rules, repeating them inappropriately in the future state.

Business rules should expose the basic business intent in a way that is as independent of the procedural mechanics of implementation as possible. We want to state that any customer having an account balance greater than $10,000 is a preferred customer. We would not, to give an extreme example, want the "rule" to be stated as "Look on the Account Profile Sheet. If the amount in box 6 is greater than $10,000, then put a check in box 10." This simple point becomes significant in considering how process and rule analysis should interact.

Consider the following hypothetical example:

A company wants to institute a process for reviewing claims automatically, to lower overhead cost by streamlining processing and minimizing the number of investigations that need to be done. They also want to be able to review this process and the rules around it to see if results can be improved, see what's working and what's not. Starting with business process modeling, they came up with the model in Figure 16.

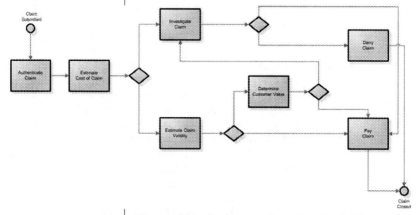

Figure 16: Business Process Model for Automated Claim Evaluation

This initial modeling of the envisioned process, while perhaps not too difficult, is also not the simplest in the world to follow; but let's walk through it. Basically, after authenticating the claim, they estimate the cost of the claim. If the estimated cost is high enough, then investigation by an agent is the only option. Below a certain point, the plan is to do some analysis-based evaluation. This begins by estimating the validity of the claim, based on a number of factors. If the probability of the claim being valid is above a certain threshold, they will pay it without further analysis. Below that level, however, they will take into account the calculated customer value (primarily a factor of claim history, modified by total revenue from client). If customer value is above a certain point, they will again simply pay the claim, provided it is above a certain estimated validity threshold. Otherwise the claim still needs to go to investigation. They will never automatically deny a claim.

When trying to identify the rules in the context of this model, and integrate them with the process flow, the rules come out looking something like this:

– If estimated claim value is at or above some X then investigation is required

– If estimated claim value is below some X then claim validity estimation is required

… and so on.

But are these really the fundamental rules? If we step back and ask what is being determined here, we see that the overall purpose of a number of these processes, acting together, is to determine what treatment to apply to a claim as shown in Figure 17.

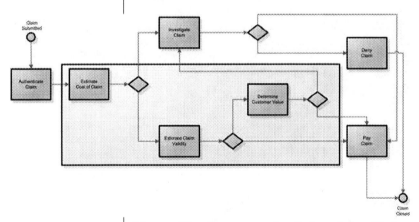

Figure 17:   Processes for Determining Claim Treatment

Specifically, we see that claim treatment is a factor of

Estimated cost of claim
Estimated claim validity
Customer value

Putting these in decision table format suddenly exposes the real underlying business rules. Looking forward, it also provides the basis for investigating which of these permutations is causing the most claims to be paid out, and so on. It also allows us to view possible other permutations that might be tested. Finally should we decide to add another factor, our process model may not change at all. We will simply add the factor to our decision table (which really represents a set of rules, each row being a rule) and which is shown in Table 3.

Table 3: Decision Table Format for Underlying Business Rules

Factors			Result
Estimated Cost of Claim	**Estimated Claim Validity**	**Customer Value**	**Claim Treatment**
Above threshold	--	--	Investigate
Not above threshold	Very high	--	Pay claim
Not above threshold	Intermediate	High	Pay claim
Not above threshold	Intermediate	Low	Investigate
Etc.			

Finally the process model is simplified to the essence of what is being accomplished from a business perspective, shown in Figure 18.

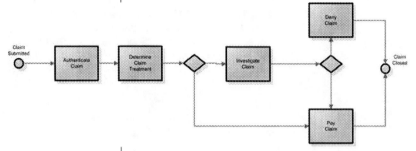

Figure 18: Simplified Claim Evaluation Process Flow

What is this telling us? It's saying that all the "steps" associated with determining claim treatment are pure information gathering and computing. There is no human activity such as "investigate" going on here, or change of actors in different locations; at least none that are really of business interest. As a result, we can easily express this whole section of "process" with rules in a declarative decision format.

It may be that there are additional rules associated with figuring out each of the contributing factors:

Estimated cost of claim

Estimated claim validity

Customer value

But again, if there is no real work flow associated with these, then rather than burn up business stakeholders' time modeling "flow" with regard to all this, we can display the dependency of claim treatment on these other rules, with a dependency diagram shown in Figure 19. In the same fashion, we would investigate these "sub-decisions" and determine in each case whether any modeling of "flow" was really required or of business interest.

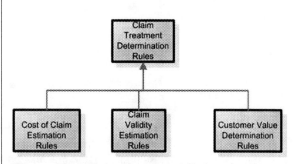

Figure 19:   Claim Treatment Determination Rule Dependencies

In system design, depending on the approach and technology being applied, perhaps flow among these various computations and decisions will have to be optimized and orchestrated. But that is really a design problem, not a business analysis problem. The simplified model exposes the essential business processes and the true, underlying business rules. It also makes the model more amenable to results measurement and adjustment, simple by adjusting rules.

In one real life example, a strictly hierarchical approach to process modeling was applied initially, with business rules placed at the bottom of the hierarchy and specified last. Qualitatively, the models were found to be overcomplicated and hard to navigate and understand. As a test, the same approach described above was applied to these models, after the fact, with business rules or rule sets integrated wherever appropriate in the business process model. The result was an over-50% reduction in the number of individual model components (e.g. processes and decision gateways) while increasing clarity from both a business and designer perspective.

What proved most effective, then, was not a top-down, process-to-rules approach, but one that iterated between both perspectives. While a full description of the approach is beyond the scope of this chapter, the essence of it was this: whenever a decision point—evaluation, computation, etc.—was encountered at any level in process analysis, a switch was made from a "process" to a "declarative" approach. That is, we asked "What factors are involved in making this decision? What else do I need to know in order to make this determination?" without regard to the mechanical process flow involved. In addition, we asked "Why do I need to know this?" to help determine whether the question being asked was itself just a component of a larger decision that was currently buried in the process flow. Asking this question also helps affirm or drive out the business motivation behind any rule or set of rules, so that traceability can be maintained and the impact of future changes in that business motivation can be rapidly assessed.

Asking these questions exposes the underlying business decisions and associated rules, which in turn affects the process model. The result is an iterative approach, going back and forth between process and rules, to uncover the optimum business model. This approach, when actually tested, produced simpler, clearer process models, exposed the essential business processes, and uncovered rules that more closely reflected the real rules of the business (as opposed to procedural "rules" associated with the details of a particular current state process implementation). As a result, these models also reflected a cleaner separation between the business model and design, clearly defining the former while minimally constraining the latter.

It's reasonable to suggest that what we've described here is simply good process modeling, and we would not dispute that. The difference is that by applying a rules perspective we were able to turn "good process modeling" into an objective, repeatable technique, one that uncovered the essential business processes while at the same time identifying the actual business rules and improving overall clarity of the business model. This was demonstrated repeatedly with experienced process modelers. This technique led to clearer, simpler processes and underlying business rules that were missed before its application. Furthermore, it helped expose procedural arbitraries and current state biases in the models.

Establishing these results and this technique also helped answer another question: Does this "rule enhanced" approach just apply in certain circumstances, or for certain kinds of systems or implementations? A commonly encountered view is that a business rules focus and business rule methods are only relevant when you're deploying rule engine technology, or when the business area is "dense" with volatile rules. While these considerations may help prioritize targets for implementing improved techniques, our experience demonstrated that creating explicit business rule work products and integrating their specification with process analysis using the described iterative technique produced clearer and more complete business models, irrespective of the business areas being considered or the technology being deployed.

The Impact of Business Rules on the Data Model

A pre-requisite for managing a portfolio of rules for precision, clarity, consistency, completeness, and reuse is a standard set of defined terms for expressing the business concepts that are used to compose the rules. In the absence of consistent terminology, none of these desired qualities for rules can be assured.

Moreover, as soon as the number of terms grows beyond a handful, and relationships between terms become numerous, subtle or intricate, some sort of modeling approach becomes necessary to precisely identify, grasp and validate all these relationships as an integrated whole.

In the business rule community, this has become known as a "fact model," expressing the "facts," or relationships among terms. Regardless of name, it is essentially a model of business information, expressed in business terms.

Traceability

It is not within the scope or intent of this chapter to talk at length about fact modeling in relation to business rules. What we do want to discuss briefly is how this model of information integrates with and impacts the data perspective of the business model. If you are familiar with this perspective, you know that you can have conceptual data models at the higher business level, logical data models at the logical system design level, and physical data models at the implementation level. There may also be an application object or class model, in some cases in lieu of the data model. Good practice requires traceability among these models, whether or not this is always done in practice.

The obvious question that comes to mind, and that needed to be addressed, is: How do we manage yet another view of information, and how does it integrate with all these other views? Have we just created a traceability nightmare? If you are serious about improving your specification, and management and reuse of business rules, you will eventually have to answer this question, especially if you are dealing with large scale systems development as we were.

As mentioned before, we were driven by pragmatics. Data traceability was already a problem. Introducing yet another view of information and information traceability requirements, besides the confusion it might generate, would simply not have been feasible. The solution was to consider the business information model (we'll use that term, since it emphasizes that this business view of information was needed, not just for the rules but to integrate with the process model as well), as an extension and detailing of the Conceptual Data Model. This meant the Conceptual Data Model became not simply a high level partitioning of data concepts for the purposes of deriving a database strategy, but a complete view of business information, from a business perspective.

In this way, the business information model—or detailed Conceptual Data Model—fit directly into the hierarchy of data analysis. It also highlighted that the business needs to understand its information in detail, not just within the context of the logical design of a particular system. The logical data model, or application model would then derive from and need to fully support the detailed business information model. As a practical point in implementing this approach, since a logical data model already existed, the business information model borrowed from and used this model as a starting point wherever possible, but departed from it where modeling abstraction, introduced for design purposes, did not support a full representation of the business.

The business information model, then, was not "traceable" to the Conceptual Data Model. It *was* the Conceptual Data Model, expressed in detail. This detail had formerly been missing in the business view of data.

It left another problem, however. The business rules expressed in terms of the business information model needed to be designed using terminology of the application design model, whether that was in terms of an application class model or a physical database design. It's not hard to see that when you throw in the logical data model, we're still talking about a lot of potential traceabilities, and that this problem of data traceability from business to design has existed all along, irrespective of rules.

Our conclusions were these:

- Depending on the application environment, whatever model is used as the basis of application design, whether an object model or physical database design, needs to be mapped to the business information model (if an object model is used, it would then have to map at some point to the physical database layer).

- The logical or application model must demonstrate fidelity to the business information model through some mapping.

- The physical database design needs to be traceable to any logical data model.

Out of the possible choices, these were considered the key traceabilities. Thus, defining the integration of business rules with the data perspective of the business model had driven us to clarify the entire mapping of data between the business model and design.

Business Rules and Improvements in Data Analysis

For terms representing key business concepts, such as *order,* where many possible "states" are potentially involved, such as incomplete, submitted, shipped, overdue, etc., an examination of these states and conditions for transitioning from one to the other is a technique sometimes applied to ensure terms or "objects" with complex or "interesting" behavior are completely understood and fully analyzed. This "state transition" analysis is commonly associated with the data or class model. Exactly how state transition diagrams fit integrate with the business model as a whole has been less evident.

With the inclusion of business rules as modeling artifacts on a par with data and process, as shown in Figure 20, the role and positioning of state transition analysis in the overall business model became much clearer. State transition analysis acts as a technique to expose further business rules, or act as a quality check on the business rules identified, in terms of completeness, correctness and consistency. The results can in turn affect the process model through the exposure of additional business rules. Thus, state transition analysis can be viewed as a business rule technique applied to data, similar to the "decision analysis" technique applied to process, and business rules became more firmly placed as the final "glue" between data and process.

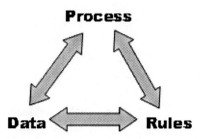

Figure 20: *Interdependency of Process Rules and Data*

Business Rules and Data Earlier in the Life Cycle

In areas where rules play predominant roles, such as customer profiling, or product/service eligibility and configuration, we found that taking this state-transition-oriented data/rule perspective very early in the life cycle can be quite effective. Looking at key entities such as customers, products and services, as a first action independent of process, examination, and states they assume, as described above, can be used to derive the first set of high level processes. This approach can help to partition and attack the complexity involved, and break the business out of its current state view of processes. From the identified states and rules, the essential process flow can be derived.

In some rule-intensive business areas, analysis began with a survey of existing systems from the perspective of key data concepts and associated rules, as an effective tool for identifying areas of overlap and for evaluating opportunity and difficulty based on an assessment of rule complexity and volume. In some projects, issues of rule consistency and underlying policy have acted as the fundamental business drivers, and were addressed first.

The Impact of Business Rules on the Data Model – Summary

Clearly business rules are closely integrated with the data view of a system, since business rules depend on a set of precisely defined and consistent set of terms. But integrating business rules into the business model also enhanced the data perspective itself by:

- Identifying and filling a gap in the data perspective by clarifying the conceptual data model as a complete, detailed view of business information

- Clarifying the traceability requirements from one information view to another

- Precisely positioning state-transition analysis and its value in the specification of the business model

- Further illuminating and organizing the relationship of process to data, through the "glue" of rules

Business Rules and Business System Requirements

In an ideal world, a complete set of requirements would be available at the commencement of a project. To achieve this objective, analysis would need to be carried out to a depth consistent with detailed logical design for all of the requirements to be fully defined. In our experience, at least for a large and complex business system, a project is developed in stages, e.g. conceptual design, logical design, and physical design. In this situation, requirements are developed and refined parallel to each phase. It is within this context that we will examine the relationship between business rules and requirements in this article.

While some people believe that business rules and business system requirements are the same, it is safer to assume that they are not, based on the definitions shown in Table 4.

Table 4:   Differences Between Business Rules and Business System Requirements

Business Rules	Business System Requirements
A business rule is a statement consisting of business terms and connecting facts that specifies business behavior, e.g. *Rule 1. If the Estimated cost of claim is not above the threshold, estimated claim validity is intermediate, and customer value is high, then pay claim; else investigate claim.*	A business system requirement is a statement of what we want the business system to perform, e.g. *The system shall determine customer claim treatment in accordance with the claim treatment rule set.*
Rule 2. etc for whole customer treatment rule set	Requirements statements are required as a basis for contractual language (what we want the developer to achieve), and are a key input to the testing process used to demonstrate that the contract has been fulfilled. The active life of a business system requirement is dependent on the life of the development contract.
The active life of a business rule is dependent on the life of the policy or procedure that contains it.	

The reason this distinction is important is that if business rules and requirements are the same, then the implication is that for every rule there must be an equivalent requirement. In a large and complex system, we could have thousands of requirements. This is an unnecessary situation since, as we will show later, a single requirement can refer to many rules, as long as they are functionally related. What is clear, then, is that rules and requirements are closely related through the business model described earlier in this chapter. To understand the relationship, we must first define what we mean by business system requirements.

Because specific business systems differ tremendously in scope, use of methodology, and the application of technology, it is necessary to define requirements using certain categories. A review of the many books written on business system requirements reveals that there is no common agreement on what these categories should be. We will adopt our own categories for the purposes of this article, as shown in Table 5. Our interest in this article is in functional requirements only.

Table 5: Categories of Business System Requirements

Functional	Non Functional
A functional requirement specifies direct user observable attributes or behaviors—also known as "outputs" of the software application—usually through output devices. It can also include manual procedures not carried by the system.	A non-functional requirement specifies application attributes or behaviors that are not directly observable by the user.
Examples of requirements included in this category are: • Process • Business performance • Organization • Location • Business Information	Examples of requirements included in this category are: • Data • Application • Technology • Security • Usability • Testability

So what is the relationship between business rules and requirements? It is a well-documented fact that a high percentage of the failures of business systems to meet the needs of the business community is directly attributable to poorly stated up-front requirements. The lack of specificity and correctness of the requirements is typically due to insufficient time being allocated to their development, and to their expression in a textual format, which in turn leads to ambiguity of understanding and interpretation. The other major problem inherent in requirements expressed in this way is that it is almost impossible for the business user to be able to certify at the beginning of the project, when requirements are developed, that they are correct and complete. Fortunately we can solve all of these problems through the use of a well-defined business model and its associated business rules.

Figure 21 shows a portion of the process model, illustrated by a process flow diagram, and its associated business rules. This model, when fully articulated, tells us everything we want to know about the business behavior that we want the business system to automate. We no longer have to struggle to specify the requirement through complex text, but can develop a simple requirement statement which references the detailed content of the business model. The requirements are now complete, consistent, unambiguous, and easily understood by both business users and system developers.

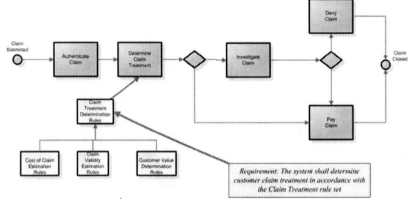

Figure 21: Requirements Made Complete by Reference to the Business Model

The lesson learned from this approach is that time spent up front in developing the business model and by reference the functional requirements is time and money saved at the back end when traditionally most of the system "problems" are uncovered during testing.

Business Rules and Testing

To demonstrate that the business system fully meets the stated business system functional and non-functional requirements, the developer and the client conduct a series of system acceptance tests. For the purposes of this article, we are interested in the testing of functional requirements that have been derived from the business model, as previously described. A good test is one that has a clear outcome, from which we can determine passing or failure of the test. The business rules and associated process model artifacts contained in business model provide the basis for effective testing.

Figure 22 is a process flow diagram which depicts the various paths that a business user can take through the process in achieving the possible business outcomes. For testing purposes we have highlighted one of the possible paths.

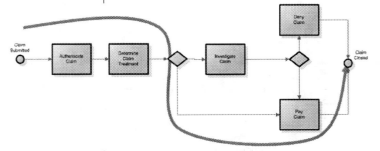

Figure 22: Path Through the Process Model of a Single Business Scenario.

Since the model contains the business rules appropriate to the selected path, we can determine the outcome by providing appropriate input values for all of the rules that will be executed along the path. As shown in Table 6, we can develop a business scenario that describes a specific instance of business behavior that we wish to demonstrate during testing. By including the input values, we can determine the expected outcome. The scenarios can then be used as the basis for specific test scripts used in the testing process.

Table 6: Business Scenarios and Testing

Scenario	Terms Evaluated
A customer submits a claim for payment for which we know the following to be true: Estimated cost of claim is not above threshold; *estimated claim validity is intermediate,* and *customer value is high.* Once authenticated, the claim is submitted to the claim treatment process for evaluation, using the claim treatment determination rule set. The above conditions are established and, as a result, the claim treatment process concludes that the claim should be paid.	Terms values evaluated are: • Estimated cost of claim = Not above threshold • Estimated claim validity = Intermediate • Customer value = High • Claim treatment = Pay Claim

The above represents a small slice of a scenario. In real life, the complete scenario would show all relevant values for the initiating event, the submitted claim, and for each process and decision point through the process thread, the inputs and expected outputs. But it at least demonstrates the concept.

Our project experience has shown that the advantage of this approach, which is based on the information contained in the business model, is that we can develop the scenarios early in the development process (no later than logical design), giving the test team valuable input on the number and complexity of tests they will be required to perform. The second advantage is that the scenarios and subsequent test scripts based on the content of the business model are readily understood by the business users, which has the benefit of removing ambiguity from the testing and acceptance process.

Summary

In our investigation of business rules, our original objective was to "simply" improve the organization's ability to clearly identify, separate out, manage its many rules, and add corresponding precision and completeness to associated system specifications. This improvement in specificity and clarity was taken more or less as a given, though our piloting efforts proved it out as well. What was less well understood and appreciated when we began was the positive impact that the insertion of separate business rule work products and techniques would have on the business model as a whole. The jury is in now, as we have described above, and we can say with some certainty that incorporating a formal approach to business rules in the business systems model:

- Improves the clarity and simplicity of business process models, and helps to expose the essential business processes and to avoid modeling arbitrary procedural details

- Helps complete and organize the data perspective of the model, determine the importance of standard terminology from a business (not database) perspective, and the key information traceabilities required.

- In adding the necessary detail to the process model, enables the creation of test scenarios and cases, partitioned and described in a way that the business can understand and validate and that can be traced to implementation level test scripts

- Clarifies the relationship of business modeling and textual requirements specification, and enables the effective integration of these two views to form a complete specification of any business system

This is good news, and probably represents a validation of one final observation: Business rules were always there in our business and/or our system models and requirements statements. They may not have been separated out or completely stated, but they were there someplace, otherwise they would not, for the most part, have been implemented at all (a nod to rogue programming). It makes sense that if business rules do represent a specific, essential component of a holistic business model, then bringing more order and rigor to that component would further clarify and organize the rest of the model and its parts, and this is exactly what we have discovered to be the case.

8 Better Rules Through Innovative Rule-Authoring Software

John Semmel

Introduction

Sometimes it starts with a directive from upper management. It may begin in state or federal legislative bodies. Other times it's just a matter of common sense. Whatever the source of the business rule, it has to be assimilated by the business people responsible for collecting and enforcing such rules, then stored in a repository, where it will be available for use in driving business processes and associated automated applications. The translation from business knowledge in someone's head to an automatable form (such as rows and columns in a database) is often the weakest link in the chain. It is this link that is fortified by rule-authoring software. The more innovative the software, the more fortified this link becomes.

This chapter tells of our journey to deliver to non-technical, business-oriented rule authors, such as underwriters, the complex task of authoring business rules ready for automation. Not only did we deliver rule-authoring software, but we also gave these authors an entire toolset, by which they can ensure that their rules are accurate, logical, and interact well within the application they support. The chapter covers:

Background

Our Medical Insurance Quotation Application is designed to allow its users maximum flexibility in configuring cost-sharing levels, usage limitations, deductibles, and so on. At the same time, this application must prevent the underwriters from selling product configurations that make no business sense. An example of a configuration that may make little sense is allowing a $40 co-pay amount for a primary care physician, and a co-pay amount of only $5 for a medical specialist. The application must also prevent underwriters from setting benefit levels that are not approved in given jurisdictions. These situations (nonsensical and restricted-product configurations) must all be addressed by our Medical Benefit Selection aspect of the application. For agility, we store all of the rules that drive Medical Benefit Selection in a database, rather than hard-code them in program code. But, this is just the beginning of delivering agility. We wanted to extend the agility deep into the rule authoring, rule analysis, and rule simulation aspects of managing the Medical Benefit Selection, and to deliver these functionalities to the non-technical, business-oriented rule authors.

According to the Rule Maturity Model (RMM), this goal is innovative, whereby such functionality represents characteristics of an organization at Level 3 of the RMM.

The amount of medical benefit selection data we collect is staggering. A single quote option may include in excess of 1,400 individual data values. Each of these values must either be selected during the quoting process or set by executing a rule.

The number of circumstances that determine what business rules are executed during medical benefit selection is also dizzying:

1. Different basic plan types have their own rules.
2. The states all regulate what we may and may not sell.
3. We offer greater flexibility to plan sponsors who are self-insured, relative to what we offer those that we insure directly.
4. There are different rules, depending on the size of the group we are insuring.
5. The rules for new business are sometimes different from those for renewals.

All together, we have ten of these factors that can influence the rules that should be executed in each case.

When we started this project, we had a data model and a rules engine. Our project team had standard database query tools and Microsoft Visual Basic. Only a few team members knew how to use these tools, as most members were from the business side of the company, not from IT.

On the other hand, we were limited only by what the data model and the rules engine could support. It was like being in a large, bare room with many cans of different-colored paints and lots of brushes, except that none of us had ever done any painting before. There were bound to be some clashes and some drips along the way.

Laying the Foundation: The Concepts and Complexity Behind the Rules

We first needed to understand the business concepts that sit behind the rules, such as plans, benefits, characteristics, and values. Our medical plans consist of *benefits*, such as Inpatient Hospitalization, which in turn consist of *characteristics* such as Co-pay Amount or Coinsurance Amount. Our *plans* define the bounds and increments of the *values* for the various characteristics. So a Physician Office Visit Co-pay Amount may assume values between $0 and $60 in five-dollar increments, for instance. The plans contain all possible values for all characteristics for all components in the plan. As a result, our plan with the 1,400 characteristics contains nearly 16,000 individual values.

As we designed and populated the database to hold the plan contents, we needed a means of verifying that the content was correct. Therefore, our first rule tool was an inquiry application. Since our plan and product data is hierarchical in nature, the inquiry tool makes heavy use of the Microsoft Windows tree view control to expose that hierarchy to the business-oriented, non-technical user. With this tool, the people who know what the plans should contain are able to inspect the plans, and to request that values be added and removed as necessary, all with no knowledge of SQL or the structure of the database. Nevertheless, the task of maintaining this data was very much a manual operation in the beginning, making it time-consuming and potentially error-prone.

While we were building plans, we were also making up the rules we would need to drive medical benefit selection. We discovered we needed four basic types of rules to fit our specific business requirements:

1. Limiting Rules: These restrict the domain of a characteristic.

2. Setting Rules: A subset of limiting rules, these restrict the domain of a characteristic to a single value.

3. Default Rules: These determine the values that show up in the drop-down lists before anything is selected. They are important because, if appropriate defaults are set, the person composing the quote may have much less work to do.

4. Non-display Rules: If the quoter can't change a value, there's no reason to clutter the page with it. Non-display rules tell the quoting application not to display the characteristic.

We now have more than thirty variations on these four rule types.

Some of these rules are driven strictly by circumstances. For example, In New Jersey, a Physician Office Visit Co-pay Amount may have certain regulated restrictions. Other rules are driven by a combination of circumstances and other selected plan values. An example in New Jersey is that a Routine Adult Physical Exam Co-pay Amount defaults to Physician Office Visit Co-pay Amount. In some rule types, the result value may be driven by two or more control values in addition to circumstances. We have situations where as many as thirty characteristics determine the value of the result in a single rule.

On top of everything else, we decided that we needed to specify a precedence among the execution of rules based on circumstances. So for instance, state-specific rules on a given characteristic need to prevent non-state-specific rules from being executed. In this way, a generic list of co-insurance values that may apply to most states can be overridden by a list that applies to a given state.

Added to the daunting complexity of this rule scheme are two pressures. First, we were under pressure to get the rules authored as soon as possible. Second, the application to implement the rules was months from being usable. To extend the painting analogy, we had to apply our paint under a strict deadline, and the room was dark.

The Learning Curve and Dealing With Rule Errors

Our first efforts at storing rules were about what you'd expect under the circumstances. The process occurred roughly as depicted in Figure 23.

Early Work Flow

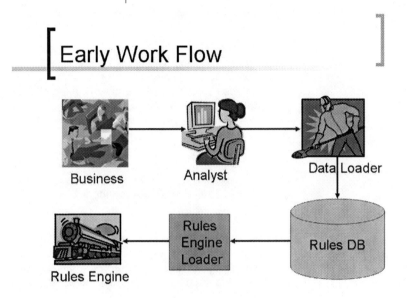

Figure 23: Original Business Rule Process

We had business people who understood the business rules—but not necessarily the rule types and interactions. These people were writing the rules in basic English sentence form. These rule authors would then pass these rules to a team of semi-technical consultants who would encode this form of the rules into spreadsheets, formatted like our database tables. Then the spreadsheets were given to data technicians who used various utilities to load the rules into the database. By the time the data, representing the translated rules, was stored, it was rife with errors. These errors resulted from the following:

1. The original English rules were sometimes incorrect or inconsistent.
2. The semi-technical consultants' interpretations of the English rules were not always correct.
3. There were technical failures loading the data.

All this led to missing data, invalid values and inconsequential data. Without a way to analyze the quality of the rules, let alone test them, we measured our progress by counting the number of rules we had produced compared to the number we estimated we needed. When we finally had an application that exercised the rules, we began to see how poor the quality of our rule data was. In the early days of testing, the poor quality of the rules was masked by the poor quality of the application itself. But, eventually, we needed to better understand the poor quality of the rules.

Because of the nature of rules, we discovered that we had more than just ordinary data problems. Individual rules are simple. But rule interactions can be quite complex. We found numerous rule conflicts where one rule would limit a characteristic's domain, say, to 1, 2 and 3 and another rule being executed at the same time would limit the same characteristic's domain to 4, 5 and 6. This, of course, is a conflict, and our application would create a null domain which caused a difficult-to-debug runtime error in our rules engine. We also found problems related to rules that unintentionally blocked other rules, due to precedence conflicts, and loads of duplicate rules.

Compounding these various problems was the time lag between when the rule was authored by the business-oriented, non-technical rule author in English and when it actually got deployed in the application. At the worst point, this could take weeks, as there were several manual steps involved. By the time the rule was deployed, the rule authors scarcely remembered what they had written.

And so, as a first defense, we developed error reports. These started out as ad hoc queries that could detect problems across the rule base as individual problems were discovered. But as more and more problems came to light, and as we began to understand the data (and rules) better, the reports became increasingly complex.

The first runs of our error reports produced overwhelming spreadsheets listing thousands of rule errors. We ran reports on a nightly basis, and the rule authors spent all day fixing the errors. Even so, no one knew at this time whether the fixed rules were correct, or even if they made business sense based on these reports. We were simply able to catch integrity issues and certain logical errors.

Our next task was to develop the ability to automatically generate a rule failure message. Some of our rules can't be "violated." Non-display and default rules are examples. A value either displays or it doesn't; the user can't place an invalid value into a field that's invisible. However, some rules can be violated. When such a violation occurs, the user is given a message describing the rule and the opportunity to change the offending value to something appropriate.

When we started authoring rules, these failure messages were coded by the rule authors themselves. We discovered that it was useful (for documentation purposes) to store the error message with the rule for all rule types, whether or not the application users would ever see it. There were some problems with this approach, however.

1. No two authors wrote failure messages the same way.
2. Some authors used inscrutable codes and abbreviations in the messages.

3. There was no way to ensure that what the error message actually represented what the rule did.

4. When an author changed the rule, there was no way to enforce that the message was changed to match the revised rule.

5. Writing the failure message was often the most time-consuming step in writing the rule.

We discovered that we could write code to read the rule data and generate failure messages from it. This gave us perfectly consistent, complete and accurate messages, and saved a great deal of the rule authors' time. The authors quickly warmed to this approach.

More and Better Software Solutions

The remainder of this chapter discusses our journey into more sophisticated and innovative software to empower the rule authors. These additional software pieces consist of:

- A rule inquiry application to enable access to and inspection of rules

- A rule maintenance application to hide the idiosyncrasies of the rules engine (and allow for changing the rules engine)

- A rule analysis application to ensure integrity of new and changed rules

- A rule application emulator so rule authors can see the rules in action (simulated with data) prior to actual deployment in the target rules engine

Our business rule process evolved roughly into that depicted in Figure 24.

Improved Workflow

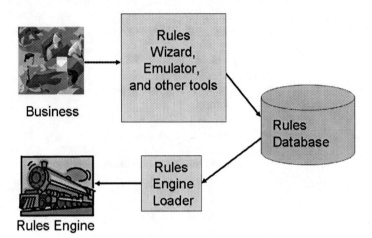

Figure 24: More Advanced Business Rule Process

The Rule Wizard

After some months of writing rules, our rule authors became more comfortable with the jargon that we created around rules and product and plan data. They began to better understand the rule types and rule interactions. It was time for us to cut out the middlemen, as it were: the people who translated the English rules to spreadsheets and those who translated spreadsheets to rows on the database.

We knew for a long time that we needed a good data-entry application to solve many of our problems. But for most of that time we were missing two ingredients:

1. The deep knowledge of our rule data structures and rule authoring business processes necessary to design such an application.
2. The resources to build and test the application.

Finally, we had advanced to the point of being ready to undertake this development effort. Rule-loading had become routine, and as a result, less time-consuming. So we diverted rule-loading time (and not a small amount of what might have been free time) to this development effort.

The inquiry application mentioned above came into play here. It had started out as a simple plan data viewer, but had gradually become more and more complex, exposing most of the static data in our database, including rules. It provided two methods for searching for rules:

1. Drilling down on a hierarchical tree view from product to component to characteristic in order to expose the rules on that characteristic.
2. Ad hoc parameter-based search for rules by rule control and result and by the circumstances under which the rules are executed.

Thus, it was logical to base the rule maintenance application on the inquiry application. Once you found a rule, you could open it up, look at it, and change it, if necessary. Opening a rule is like opening any document under Microsoft Windows. The maintenance application we designed followed the model we had built around writing our business rules.

Our rules engine was, and is, a versatile piece of software. It would have been possible to have encoded rules directly into this engine. These rules would have looked like discrete conditional statements, rules at their lowest level, or like rule assembler code. But this task would have been highly technical and painstaking, a job most of the business-oriented, non-technical rule authors would have been hard-pressed to undertake.

So, even before we created a rule maintenance facility, we built two layers between these rule authors and the rules engine. This is a database in which to store a relational representation of the rule data, and an interface program that translated the rules from the database into the language of the target rules engine. This worked well for two reasons:

1. It allowed us to model rules our own way (in the eyes of the business-oriented authors), letting the interface program mediate the difference between the way the authors viewed rules and the way the rules engine wants and needs to view them.

2. If we ever wanted to change to a different rules engine (or add a different one to our technology set), we'd still have our logical rule data encoded in our database.

And so, we developed another tool, our Rule Wizard, as a third layer between the rule authors and the rules engine. It hides many of the details of the data model used to store the rules, and otherwise facilitating the storage of valid rules.

The first task for a rule author is to establish the kind of rule to author. The kind of rule determines how the Rule Wizard operates, because each rule type has its own unique data requirements. The Rule Wizard includes a decision tree that takes the rule author through a series of questions and answers to determine what type of rule to use in a given instance.

The second task for the rule author is to specify circumstances under which the rule is to be executed. Some of these circumstances also determine what other rule specifications might be required or optional in the given rule.

Our Rule Wizard has access to the plan data regulated by the rules. So if the author is specifying valid values for a Specialist Co-pay Amount for a given plan, the author can select from only the co-pay values assigned to the Specialist in that plan. This makes almost impossible the kinds of mistakes that were frequent in early rule loading.

Before a rule is stored, the Rule Wizard analyzes the quality and integrity of the rule:

1. A full referential integrity check on the rule performs edits that would be impractical to do screen-to-screen interactively, and includes edits that can only be performed once the rule is fully coded.

2. A check for rule conflicts detects those circumstances for which the current rule, along with another existing rule, will create an empty domain.

3. A duplicate rule check prevents exact rule duplicates from being stored.

4. A blocking rule check detects rules that will block the current rule, and for rules the current rule will block.

5. There is automatic generation of a failure message for the rule.

The delivery of the Rule Wizard not only resulted in a huge advancement in enabling the rule authors to write rules, but the rule authors could now easily address rule quality and integrity, all without much technical support. They can find their rules, open them, inspect them and change them. They could do so safely, knowing that quality issues among the rules would be detected automatically. New rules were now very easy to write. And, best of all, it was difficult to create an invalid rule.

Wizards Are Us

Following the success of the Rule Wizard, we developed other data maintenance and validation tools along the same lines that worked against other static data tables in our database. All of these applets hang from the same tree, the inquiry tool we started out with in the beginning. We now have nine of these maintenance components. The Rule Wizard is by far the most complex of them.

Application Emulation

But there was still a major problem. Once the rule was written, it had to be loaded into the rules engine. Then the rules engine had to be deployed on a server before the authors could see their rules in action. This could take a few days. Then, if there was a problem with the rules, the authors had no means for diagnosing the problem. Developers familiar with the rules engine would have to dig into the problem and tell the authors the rules that were in conflict. Then once the rules were fixed, it took a few more days before they could be retested.

This is a huge problem for two reasons. First, it was highly inefficient to let a defect get so far along in the process without being addressed. Second, the rule authors were not easily learning the craft of authoring rules because feedback was so slow.

Entering an entire quote is a time-consuming process consisting of several steps other than medical benefit selection. And, as stated, the application provided no diagnostics on rules that were of any use to the authors. So we next wrote and delivered an Application Emulator that isolated medical benefit selection and provided feedback on the rules that were being executed as the emulator ran. This emulator could load newly written rules in a local copy of the rules engine database, so the authors didn't have to wait for the nightly load before they could test. Now the rule authors could see both what the end users would see as well as all of the rules driving the application.

But, this still wasn't perfect. At first, the emulator had no means of displaying the non-display characteristics, so the authors had no means of knowing what was going on behind the scenes for these characteristics. The emulator is not a particularly fast application. And while it reliably shows how rules will be executed in the application, it doesn't provide any additional logical support, such as flagging duplicate rules, or indicating when a default value is not in the valid domain set for a characteristic. Neither of these conditions cause problems in the application, but they are both logical inconsistencies that should be addressed.

Ongoing Efforts

From the very beginning, our quotation application has been a moving target. The healthcare industry is changing rapidly: HMOs are on their way out; HSAs are on their way in. This has meant racing to develop the base quotation application while trying to keep up with a barrage of new business requirements that were unknown when development started. For our rules environment, this has required a high degree of flexibility.

1. We have added new rule types on several occasions. More than a third of our 34 rule types were invented after we started writing rules. The newer rule types have tended to be more complex in nature than some of the early types.

2. We have changed our notion of rule precedence on a couple of occasions.

3. When we started, each rule had only one set of circumstances under which it would be executed, although those sets might be very complex. Now we allow for the definition of multiple groupings of circumstances under which each rule will be executed.

4. We've created rule cloning facilities so that rule authors can create whole categories of rules without having to enter them individually.

As far as we've come with authoring tools, it isn't far enough. Our Application Emulator is not integrated with our Rule Wizard, so the authors have to go from one application to the other to enter and test their rules. Testing can be a grueling process as there are an astronomical number of possible sets of circumstances, each set having its own mix of rules.

We are also still grappling with the rule set migration issue. When we build rules into our rules engine, we do so for entire plans at once. This means that all the rules must be written and working at the same time. What we'd like to be able to do is to include rules in the rules engine selectively, so that we can hold some rules in development status while other rules get moved along to production. This is a rule author issue to an extent, as the authors must be the ones to manage which rules go and which do not for a given rules engine build.

This issue is being addressed with a migration facility that has been developed, but is not yet in use.

Timeline

In retrospect, parts of this process came together quickly. At the time it was happening, it seemed endless. It's instructive to look back at how this project progressed.

- 4th Quarter 2002:

    - Defined product and plan data

- 2nd Quarter 2003:

    - Started product and plan data load

    - Defined rules

    - Started rules load

    - Improved inquiry tool (ongoing)

- 3rd Quarter 2003:

    - Continued product load

    - Continued rules load

    - Rules engine/UI in final development

    - Application is due at the end of July!

- 3rd Quarter 2003:

    - Integrity and conflict reports

- 4th Quarter 2003:
  - Duplicate reports
  - Failure message generation
  - Rule Wizard development begins
- 1st Quarter 2004:
  - Rule Wizard deployed
  - Dental plans implemented (not many rules)
- 2nd Quarter 2004:
  - Product, Plan and other Wizards deployed
  - First Medical Flex Plan Pilot implemented!
- 3rd Quarter 2004:
  - Rule Emulator deployed
- 1st Quarter 2005:
  - Planning begins for a migration facility
- 2nd Quarter 2005 through 4th Quarter 2005
  - Upgrades to Rule Wizard and other data maintenance tools
  - Upgrades to Rule Emulator
  - More Medical Plans in production
- 1st Quarter 2006
  - Migration facility deployed
  - Start of migration to VB.NET

Conclusions and Summary

We now have nearly 100,000 rules sitting in our database, guiding Medical Benefits Selection, all managed by the true rule authors.

But our odyssey into rule authoring is by no means over. In our end vision, rules will be even easier to enter than they are now. Our testing software will automatically examine a rule as it will be executed in all possible circumstances, and will ferret out all conflicts and inconsistencies between the current rule and others in the rule database. It may even offer to mediate these conflicts and inconsistencies.

Rule deployment will be improved too. It still takes an overnight job to get a newly authored rule into the rules engine for use by our application in a development environment. It can still take weeks to reach production, which is fine for certain kinds of projects, but not for problem fixes. Some of our business partners are very forward thinking on this, and are demanding the ability to get rules into production overnight.

I'll close with a list of the insights I've gained in working through the process of supporting a rules-based application.

1. The people with the deep business knowledge are the best people to author the rules, even rules targeted for automation. The process of translating their rules through intermediaries leads to mistakes and misinterpretations.

2. You can't go any faster than you can go, even with tools. If you are an organization new to business rules, allow time for rule authors to learn their new trade and use their new tools. There will be stages of rework as the rule authors and related tools evolve in their maturity. Deliver prototypes along the way.

3. The rules may never be perfect, but refinements and improvements are a part of the ongoing process. This is a sign of great success. In

some cases, conflicts encountered in rule authoring spring from conflicts inherent in the business process, conflicts that were not apparent (or were at least undocumented) until the process was deconstructed and loaded into a logical system.

4. There is something to be said for starting with a manual approach to loading rules into a database. Rule authors need to understand what rules are, what their pieces are (such as plans, characteristics, values), and what the process consists of when moving from conceiving of a rule, determining its type, determining its execution circumstances, and validating its integrity. There's nothing to systematize until you have a manual system that is defined and understood.

5. Rules are no good if you can't find them. They might as well be buried in code if they are buried in a database.

6. The shorter the time between when the rule is written and when the rule is tested with other rules in the target environment, the more immediate the feedback to the rule authors, the faster they learn their trade, and the fewer mistakes they make in rule set-up. Back in the day when programs had to be punched onto cards and run in batches, it was very hard to learn how to write and test code. Now, a line of code can be written one moment, and tested in debug mode the next. This is also the ideal kind of environment for developing rules.

7. Individual rules are simple, but interactions between rules are complex and numerous. Tools are required to explore these interactions.

8. When rule systems become as complex as program code, you need separate but equal parallel environments in which to develop each. The code must be tested against a known good copy of the rules, and the rules must be tested against a known good copy of the code, or it becomes very difficult to find the source of problems.

9. The rule authors are the most important people in the equation. This means finding the right people and giving them the proper training and IT support.

It should be fun to be a rule author, in the same way that it's fun to do crossword puzzles or to play chess. Each business requirement is a logical problem to solve using the innovative rule authoring software. What makes this work drudgery is not the logical analysis involved, but the tediousness of the work in encoding and testing the solution to a given business requirement. While rule authoring software will never compete with video games for entertainment value, it should strive to give the authors satisfaction in their work by allowing them to go from concept to realization as smoothly and as rewardingly as possible.

Part III
The Technology Side of Business Rules

For the more technical audience, this section explores the role of rule architecture and rule architects, and delivering rules in state-of-the-art technology. It covers insights into the role of the rule architect on a systems development project (Chapters 9 and 10), delivering business rules at an enterprise level (Chapter 11), achieving advanced rule maturity with BRMS technology at a major corporation (Chapter 12), how business rule management leads to an enterprise policy hub (Chapter 13), and a current option in rule management software that is not tied to a particular BRMS (Chapter 14).

Again, in their own words, each author selects quotes to provide the reader with insights into each chapter:

"Organizing thousands of rules, even hundreds of rules, is a challenging task. The people, the process, and the tool are three key factors for the success of the task, just as with accomplishing any other challenging task. Therefore, this chapter covers: role of the rule architect, relationship of the rule architect to other architects, BPMS and BRMS, how best to write a rule, and how to express and organize rules in sets."

Chapter 9, Gene Weng

"In today's growing global market where American companies are outsourcing their key services and components, it is urgent for the technology and business operation managers to understand the risks involved in offshore outsourcing. The core of a business is its business rules, which need to be protected from deliberate or accidental misuse. A well-defined business rules methodology, focused on business goals and objectives, addresses most of the concerns."

Chapter 10, May Abraham

"While the promise of BRMS is alluring, realizing the benefits requires more than finding rules and integrating a business rule engine....As [business rule] applications proliferate, it will be necessary to provide stewardship and governance to support intelligent and consistent use of the technology. This is particularly true for those organizations that wish to truly embrace the Business Rules Approach and support multiple business-driven projects, both individually and at an enterprise level."

Chapter 11, Brian Stucky

"The ongoing ability to modify the business rules used to deliver results to the customers is a significant competitive advantage for Equifax. Once customers are exposed to the capabilities the rule-driven system offers, they gain a world of new opportunities."

Chapter 12, Linda Nieporent

"The greatest ROI becomes possible when automating and improving operational decisions across the enterprise…the conversion of insight into action through embedding executable rules and models directly into the decision services used by applications. These models might be predictive scorecards, decision trees, neural nets or rules derived from genetic algorithms. This is where the future lies, bringing true business intelligence to operational decision-making… One of the great advantages to an enterprise policy hub is that it adds value to and works with core technology trends, not against them."

Chapter 13, James Taylor

"For the knowledge part [of RMM Level 2], the source rule repository needs to store rules, at least in business-friendly form, with terms and rule clauses and grouped by decisions. But for the agility part, the source rule repository must enable fast rule changes. Fast rule changes are possible to the technical rules in the BRMS, but the impact of those changes on the business requires metadata and traceability at business fingertips."

Chapter 14, Barbara von Halle

9 The Role of the Rule Architect in Organizing Thousands of Rules

Gene Weng

Introduction

Organizing thousands of rules, even hundreds of rules, is a challenging task. The people, the process, and the tool are three key factors for the success of the task, just as with accomplishing any other challenging task. Therefore, this chapter covers:

- Introducing the role of the rule architect

- Architecture: General

- Architecture: Rule-specific

- Relationship of the rule architect to other architects

- BPMS and BRMS

- How best to write a rule

- How to express rules in sets

- How to organize rule sets

- Summary

- Suggested topics to explore further

- References

Introducing the Role of the Rule Architect

First, a rule architect role should be established in the team; second, a rule architecture document should be one of the deliverables in the whole development process, and third, proper tools should be chosen for designing and documenting the rule architecture. The Business Rules Approach can be viewed as an application of the divide-and-conquer technique. By separating decision logic from application logic, business rules help reduce the complexity of any enterprise information system. However, a rule-based system can still be very complicated if there are hundreds or thousands of rules, even though an individual rule looks very simple. Without well-designed rule architecture, the overall decision rationale will be hard to understand and manage. The system will be hard to maintain. Integration with the rest of the system is also non-trivial. Well-designed rule architecture will help the overall system to meet these challenges.

Architecture: General

Software architecture as a concept came out in the 1960's, but has increased in popularity since the early 1990's, due to the greatly increased complexity of large software systems. The Wikipedia article "Software Architecture" provides a short but comprehensive introduction.[27]

Software architecture can be viewed from different perspectives: as representation, as process and as design. In this chapter, I'll focus on the design aspect.

---

27. Wikipedia.org, Software Architecture, http://en.wikipedia.org/wiki/Software_architecture

System architecture, infrastructure architecture, application architecture, and data architecture are typical architectures in enterprise information systems. Rule architecture is another member of the family if a Business Rules Approach is applied.

Goal, requirement, constraint and assumption are major concepts associated with architecture. From the design perspective, goals are a set of objectives for the architecture to achieve. Requirements must be satisfied by the architecture design; they can be functional and non-functional. Functional requirements are business-specific. Non-functional requirements include performance, fault-tolerance, backward compatibility, forward compatibility, scalability, extensibility, reliability, maintainability, availability, serviceability, and usability. In many cases, architecture design is constrained by a certain number of factors, such as existing legacy systems. These constraints limit design choices. Architectural assumptions further exclude other options.

From the design perspective, an architect's task is to come up with an architecture specification based on goals, requirements, assumptions and constraints. Unfortunately, in many cases, there is no optimal solution. Optimizing one aspect will have a negative impact on another aspect. For example, a complex algorithm may be used to optimize performance. But the maintainability may be more difficult due to the complexity of the algorithm. Therefore, an architect carries out an architectural trade-off analysis.

The following steps serve as the guidance for the process of designing an architecture.

1. Define quality aspects, such as performance, maintainability etc.
2. Prioritize quality aspects. Which aspect has more weight? It will help make a decision when conflicts exist.
3. Come up with different design options. Always try to think of alternatives. No alternative means no choice.

4. Determine which design to use.

Architecture: Rule-Specific

Although the discussion on general architecture also applies to rule architecture, rule architecture has its own specific characteristics. Article 9 of The Business Rules Manifesto indicates business rules are "Of, By, and For Business People, Not IT People."[28] Rule architecture should be business friendly.

One of the advantages of a Business Rules Approach is its simplicity. This simplicity allows your business rule applications to achieve two important goals that traditional applications are not able to: simplicity and agility.

Code base vs. Rule Base

The code base (e.g., SQL, VB, C/C++, Java, COBOL, etc.) in traditional applications is not easy to understand, even by technical developers. On the other hand, a rule base (i.e., a set of atomic executable rules) is much more comprehensible. With a rule base, developers will not only understand the results of a decision (driven by rules), but also the reasons for the results (i.e., the conditions of the related rules).

System Execution Performance vs. System Development Performance

In many cases, response time is an important performance requirement for system execution. But the system development performance, i.e. the time for developing a new system and for making changes to the existing system, is becoming more and more important. Business rates of change cannot tolerate long system changes anymore. An easy-to-understand, straightforward design is often a better choice. Therefore, a rule architect not only

---

28. Business Rules Group, *The Business Rules Manifesto*, Article 9. http://www.businessrulesgroup.org/brmanifesto.htm

needs to be sensitive to system execution performance, but should also pay equal, if not more, attention to the system development performance.

Business Intuitive vs. System Thinking

Any software system, including a rule-based system, is a formalization, or abstraction of the real world. The Business Rules Approach allows business analysts and business rule analysts to participate in the entire process of system development. Though in many cases business intuition may suggest a viable system design, business intuition should not replace critical system design thinking and good software engineering principles.

Relationship of the Rule Architect to Other Architects

The rule architect should work with other architects to define interfaces so that rules interact with the rest of the system. The following is a list of considerations in design.

1. Coupling with the rest of the system

Rule services can be embedded, tightly coupled, or loosely coupled. For example, a rule service can be a Java object called by another Java object (embedded). Rule service can be a Java Session Bean called by a Java client (tightly-coupled), or it can be invoked as a web service through messaging (loosely-coupled).

2. Rule service granularity

A rule architect must work with application architects or business process architects to agree upon the granularity of the rule services. One end of the spectrum is that each rule set is a rule service. The other end is all rule sets are organized by a rule flow and the rule flow provides rule services. Application developers who use rule services get maximum flexibility in the first case. But it brings challenges to rule developers: it's harder to enforce policy consistency. By contrast, the second case gives application developers minimum flexibility but makes it easier for rule developers to enforce policy consistency. In most cases, the desired design will fall between the two extremes.

3. API Intensive vs. Scenario Intensive

In many cases, rule services are coarse-grained. That means that there are not many APIs (Application Programming Interface) for rule services. However, rule services are likely to be scenario-intensive. For example, if a rule set evaluates 8 variables, then it has 256 different scenarios in the simplest case: every variable only takes *true* and *false*. A rule architect could use key scenarios to communicate with the service users. A key scenario consists of primary variables and corresponding primary values that are most significant to the business. For example, to determine a reasonable coverage amount for a life insurance policy, a set of rules could use a number of variables such as coverage amount, age of insured, is the insured a smoker, etc. A sample key scenario might be a coverage amount of one million dollars for a 40-year-old person with certain characteristics.

4. Data Model

A data model specifies the data within the domain that rules need to reference. Rule base systems work best with certain kinds of data model or database designs than others. For example, object and XML are two major approaches for specifying data in hierarchical fashion. The rule architect needs to understand that, from a rule perspective, a flatter hierarchy (that is, fewer levels) is usually better than a deeper one (that is, lots of levels). Navigating a deep hierarchy may necessitate multiple nested loops. Thus, the logic of the rules becomes difficult to understand and to maintain. A rule architect should communicate strong preferences in data structures to the data architects as early as possible.

BPMS and BRMS

Recently, both BPMS (Business Process Management Systems) and BRMS (Business Rule Management Systems) are increasingly interesting to enterprise information system developers.

Three Scenarios for BPMS and BRMS

Consider three scenarios for a target system: only process-intensive, only decision- intensive, both process- and decision-intensive.

If the system is process-intensive only, (i.e. it does not have many rules), then a BPMS product may suffice, because most BPMS products provide some support for rules. However, BPMS vendors usually provide very limited support for rules, compared with rules support provided by BRMS software.

If the target system is decision-intensive only, (i.e. it does not have complex process flows), then a BRMS product may suffice. Most BRMS products support the concept of rule flows, which are needed for complex decisions. Also, rule flows can be used to implement process flows. However, most BRMS products only provide limited process flow support, compared with process flow support provided by BPMS software.

The most interesting and challenging case, naturally, is the third scenario: both process- and decision-intensive. In this case, it's still possible to deploy BPMS software only, or BRMS software only. The problem with using BPMS software only is that the rules are not separated from the process; hence, the process flows will be represented in a much more complicated way. The resulting process flows are hard to understand and manage. The problem with using BRMS software only includes its limited support of the process flow management.

Some vendors provide integrated software for both of business process management and business rule management. Most vendors only provide one solution. However, many BPMS vendors have established strategic partnerships with BRMS vendors, and vice versa. These partnerships allow you to integrate the specific strengths of BPMS software and BRMS software, although you need to assess the corresponding technology integration issues.

Regardless of your underlying software selection, a rule architect must work with the process architect to clearly define the relationship between rule architecture and process architecture.

The Rule Architect in a BPMS Environment

BPMS and the representation of business processes are gaining popularity as the logical view for system integration, especially in the service-oriented systems. On the other hand, BRMS is never designed to be used as an integration platform. From a system perspective, BRMS is seen as the platform needing to be integrated. This does not mean that the rule architect should not have a global view of the system. Instead, rule architects should work with business process architects or application architects closely to enforce business policy consistency across processes.

How Best to Write a Rule

A rule architect should also provide guidance to rule developers on the best way to express rules, in much the same way that data architects provide guidance on the best way to express data access requests using SQL (Structured Query Language). In both cases, some expressions that are semantically equivalent will perform better than others.

For example, rule developers should typically avoid mixing "AND" and "OR" in a rule condition because doing so makes the rule harder to understand, and therefore harder to maintain. A better approach is to reduce such a rule to a set of ORs.

For example, following this guideline, the rule below

    if   A and

        (B or (C and D))

    then E

can be restated as

    if   (A and B) or

        (A and C and D)

    then E

How to Express Rules in Sets

Rule statements, decision tables, and decision trees are metaphors, or popular ways to organize and represent a rule set. Decision tables and decision trees provide natural graphical view of rules. Readers can find more information about decision tables on http://en.wikipedia.org/wiki/Decision_table[29] and decision trees on http://en.wikipedia.org/wiki/Decision_Tree.[30] The following diagrams are also from Wikipedia:

Printer troubleshooter

Conditions	Printer does not print	Y	Y	Y	Y	N	N	N	N
	A red light is flashing	Y	Y	N	N	Y	Y	N	N
	Printer is unrecognized	Y	N	Y	N	Y	N	Y	N
Actions	Check the power cable				X				
	Check the printer-computer cable	X			X				
	Ensure printer software is installed	X			X		X		X
	Check/replace ink	X	X			X	X		
	Check for paper jam		X		X				

Figure 25: Sample Decision Table

29. Wikipedia.org, Decision Table, http://en.wikipedia.org/wiki/Decision_table
30. Wikipedia.com, "Decision Tree," http://en.wikipedia.org/wiki/Decision_Tree.9

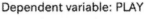

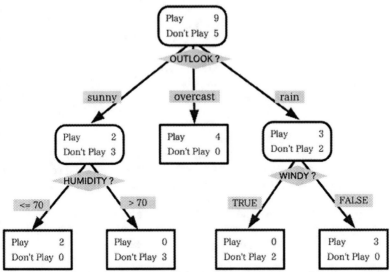

Figure 26: Sample Decision Tree

Decision tables (Figure 25) and decision trees (Figure 26) not only make rule creation and modification easier, but also help human beings understand rules, and discover gaps in the rule set logic. Data mining algorithms and statistical modeling tools sometimes serve as sources of business rules, facilitated by the fact that decision trees are often the output of data mining algorithms and statistical modeling tools. Due to the benefits as described above, always try to consider organizing rules into a decision table or decision tree.

Unfortunately, not all BRMS products support these metaphors (decision tables, decision trees), especially in the rule-base reporting functionality. Even when these metaphors are supported, many BRMS product automatically translate rules in these forms into regular rule statements when rules are saved into the rule base or executed. In such cases, representing rules as decision tables and decision tree in the design document is still beneficial.

How to Organize Rule Sets

A rule architect should organize rules into sets based on a well-considered meaningful theme. This theme could be result-oriented (e.g., includes all rules that determine the value of a single variable), or condition-oriented (e.g., includes all rules that determine the values of many variables but have the same/similar condition), or business-specific grouping (e.g., by business line).

As an example, a result-oriented rule set may contain only rules that determine whether a customer is qualified for a discount. This is the most common way to organize rules into well-defined rule sets.

A condition-oriented rule set may contain rules having "order amount" in all of their conditions. In such a rule set, order amount is used as a major factor to determine multiple outputs: eligibility of rebate, discount percentage and eligibility of free shipping etc.

The size of the rule set is another important consideration for design. Though there is no upper bound for the rule set size, a rule set with more than 25 rules is typically less manageable.

Rule Set Dependency Diagram

Individual rules are easy to change. The hard part is to make sure the change does not cause undesirable or unexpected side effects, due to the dependency among rules. Therefore, it is critical for a rule architect to draw diagrams of rule set dependency.

Definition: Rule set B depends on rule set A if

1. Rule set A sets the value of a variable X and rule set B uses the variable X in its condition, as shown in Figure 27 or
2. Both rule sets A and B set the value for same variable X, as shown in Figure 28.

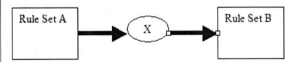

Figure 27:   Rule Set A Sets the Value of X and Rule Set B Uses It

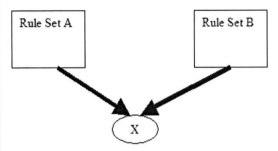

Figure 28:   Rule Sets A and B Set the Value for X

An overall diagram of rule set dependency can be drawn based on the definitions above.

The overall rule set dependency diagram is different from the rule flow diagram.   The rule flow design should follow the constraints defined in the diagram of the rule set dependency.   Theoretically, many rule flows are possible, given a rule dependency diagram, unless the diagram is linear.   Therefore, rule dependency diagram can highlight more flexibility to rule flow/business process design.

Aggregate Rules Based on Change Likelihood

If maintainability and time-to-market are high priorities, one way to achieve these design goals is to reduce the number of rule sets that need to change. In many cases, not every rule is equal in the sense of future change. Some rules are more stable than others.

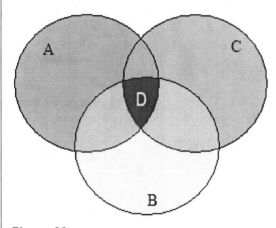

Figure 29:

Figure 29 shows that three rule sets, A, B and C, contain rules which have variable X in their conditions or outcomes. If the variable X is not stable, i.e., change requests related to X are frequent, then an alternative design could reduce the number of rule set changes. One alternative design has 4 rule sets: D, A-D, B-D, C-D, where rule set D is the intersections of A and B and C. In this way, one rule set change is needed instead of three.

Summary of the Chapter

This chapter serves as an introduction to rule architecture and the important role of the rule architect. Rule architecture is a special case of the software application architecture. Therefore general principles of the software application architecture also apply to rule architecture. Rule architecture should be business-friendly, meaning that it should help the business better understand, manage, maintain and update decision logic. From a system perspective, the rule architect should leverage strength of the Business Rules Approach: simplicity and agility.

Important guidelines from this chapter for the reader are:

- The rule architect is a critical role on a rule-based systems development team.

- The rule architect should be closer to the business thinking than other types of architects.

- The rule architect should be concerned with system development and maintenance performance, not just system execution performance.

- The rule architect is a key player in influencing important architectural decisions, including the coupling and granularity of rule services, optimal data structure design, selection of BPMS and BRMS products, writing rules, organizing rule sets, and representing rule sets.

This chapter is not a rule architecture methodology. Instead, it provides a few examples to rule architects as inspiration in their architectural thinking.

Suggested Topics to Explore Further

1. Architectural challenges when moving to upper levels of the Rule Maturity Model.
2. Architectural impact of emerging standards such as the semantics of business vocabulary and business rules specification (SBVR).

References

Business Rules Group, *The Business Rules Manifesto,* Article 9.
http://www.businessrulesgroup.org/brmanifesto.htm

Wikipedia.com, "Decision Table,"
http://en.wikipedia.org/wiki/Decision_table

Wikipedia.com, "Decision Tree,"
http://en.wikipedia.org/wiki/Decision_Tree

Wikipedia.com, "Software Architecture,"
http://en.wikipedia.org/wiki/Software_architecture

Wikipedia.com, "Software Architecture,"
http://en.wikipedia.org/wiki/Software_architecture

10 Building a Business Rules Architecture that Will Stand the Test of Time

May Abraham

The Climate of Today's Global Market Requires a Business Rules Architecture

In today's growing global market where American companies are outsourcing their key services and components, it is urgent for the technology and business operation managers to understand the risks involved in offshore outsourcing. The article, "Managing the Risks of Offshore IT Outsourcing,"[31] written by Steven R. Pozzi, senior vice president of Chubb & Son and chief underwriting officer for Chubb Commercial Insurance is an eye opener. Pozzi writes that companies that outsource information technology (IT) functions may face lawsuits if they don't take steps to protect non-public personal information. "If an employee of the contracting firm steals or misuses confidential or personal information that causes a violation of U.S. privacy regulations, the U.S.-based client would be the likely target of any lawsuits," he writes. "Outsourcing contractors must meet U.S. and

---

31. Pozzi, Steven R., "Managing the Risks of Offshore IT Outsourcing," computerworld.com/action/article.do?command=printArticleBasic&articleId=9000673

foreign mandates relating to privacy legislation and public disclosure laws, such as the Sarbanes-Oxley Act."

The question is: how can companies manage the risk when most of your business components are maintained and developed in overseas places like India, China, and Eastern Europe?

In recent years, business rules and related service components have been gaining visibility and importance, both in the business and information technology world. Experience proves that the abstraction and isolation of the business logic from other parts of the system enables business areas to codify, maintain and manage rules as a reusable component of the application environment. A Business Rules Approach helps mitigate the risk and helps build technology services and business products with better service quality and security. The core of a business is its business rules, which need to be protected from deliberate or accidental misuse. A well-defined business rules methodology, focused on business goals and objectives, addresses most of the concerns. This Business Rules Approach needs to be driven by the company's operations managers, and supported by a structured methodology aimed at managing their core business knowledge. From this Business Rules Approach should emerge an appropriate business rules architecture for the organization. This chapter covers:

- Delivering product strategy through business rules

- What is business rules architecture?

- Process, rules, objects and how they work together

- How to identify a rule vs. non-rule

- Guidelines for the business rule acquisition phase

- Where and how to find business rules

- Business rule analysis guidelines

- Business rule implementation guidelines
- Guidelines for defining an enterprise business rules architecture
- Business rule design guidelines
- Roles and responsibilities of individuals involved in business rules architecture
- The business process and rules architect
- The business rules technical analyst
- Systems integration engineer
- The controversy of who owns the business rules
- Summary

Delivering Product Strategy Through Business Rules

An appropriate business rules architecture can prove critical today in meeting a company's marketing strategy, for example, enabling the introduction of new products faster and in a cost-effective way.

For instance, an insurance company can model the underwriting process and facilitate the implementation of newly defined insurance products using business rules. After all, such a product is a way of packaging coverages, benefits, limitations, exclusions and cost in a way that meets a market need. Each component of a product has its own rules, and these rules vary from state to state. An appropriate business rules architecture can lay the foundation for product structure for various lines of businesses and allow for the dynamic configuration of new products. Business rules can serve as the building blocks for various business components. Once these basic components and their associated rules are in place, they can be packaged in various configurations to form new products within a given product line.

Business Rule Management Systems (BRMS) assist organizations in implementing business rules services. Used appropriately, a BRMS allows a business user to better understand and, sometimes manage a subset of the business rules, and perform sophisticated rule-related tasks. The latter may include conducting "what if" analysis and regression testing before a product is released. These systems also support the prototyping of business scenarios, through rules, before the actual system is built. These techniques can be very useful for the business managers in their strategic planning efforts.

What is Business Rules Architecture?

Loosely speaking, business rules architecture is the foundation by which an organization will manage its business rules. This involves building a business rules architecture that makes sure the business rules support business objectives and goals and can change on demand, as needed. For the purpose of this chapter, business rules architecture is the business rule foundation established by a business rules architect so that the collection of rules, at any time, is well-understood and performs appropriately. If sufficient consideration is not given to the business rules architecture, the business rules can be in danger of being lost to the business, inconsistent, or perform poorly in target technology. So, it is important to understand the scope of the business rules architecture and to define its pieces before beginning the business rule acquisition. For enterprise-wide rules, a proper business rules architecture is even more important. Aspects of the business rules architecture are:

- Identification of target rule sets (even before you know the rules!) and hierachical relationship among them, if appropriate

- Depiction of rule flow among related rule sets

- Naming conventions for rules, terms, and rule sets

- Templates for how to instantiate (express instances of a kind of rule) so that different rule analysts express the similar rules in the same way

- An understanding of which kinds of rules are implemented in which kinds of technology

Process, Rules, Objects and How They Work Together

Business rules are statements that define or constrain some aspect of a business process. They govern the way a business process is performed, and implement the business or regulatory procedures and policies. Business rules dynamically determine the outcome of a decision-making process, and describe the structure and relationships among business concepts.

Business rules are different from business objects, though both exist within an application. Business objects represent business entities (e.g., customers, products, etc.). Business rules implement the policies and practices of an organization, and control the ways that business objects perform business functions. Without business rules, business objects would have a hard-coded value for business credit, for example. Using business rules, the system can "reason" a value based on complex and timely criteria. These criteria and rules may vary from one customer to another or, in time, can often be changed in line with business policy changes. Some examples where business rules apply are:

- Whether to increase customer credit

- Whether to offer a customer a new product

- Whether to create a new product

- Determine exceptions within a process

- Determine applicant ineligibility
- Determine eligibility for special product features.

Analysis of a business operation always starts with articulating the business process. The process has a flow (a workflow), and within the workflow are discrete steps. Throughout the process there are business rules. Whether the rules are about *how* work must be processed, *where* work must go, or *who* is qualified to process work, business rules are key to the process. Business rules guide the process toward acceptable outcomes or to exceptions needing special attention.

How to Identify Rules vs. Non-rules

Following the Business Rules Approach, business and systems requirements should not contain buried rules. Instead, the rules should be separated, but connected to other kinds of requirements. Harvesting of rules may include careful study of all versions of the business requirements documents and the systems requirement documents, in addition to discussions with the business experts.

What is Considered a Business Rule?

Any statement that enforces relationships among data, enforces the collection of valid data required to perform a business sub-process, or monitors the correct execution of a business sub-process is a candidate business rule.

The natural language itself can give clues about which statements might be business rules. Often, statements that contain the following words can indicate business rules:

Action words:

ASSESS, DIAGNOSE, COMPARE, EVALUATE, DECIDE, VALIDATE, DETERMINE, VERIFY.

More clues:

ALL, NEVER, ALWAYS, NONE, ONLY, ALTHOUGH, SHOULD, CAN, SOME, EVERY, UNLESS, EXCEPT, UNTIL

IF, IMPLIES, MAY, MUST, WHOEVER, WHENEVER, WITH/WITHOUT.

What is Not Considered a Business Rule?

Statements that do not fit into the above categories are not likely to represent business rules, such as steps in business sub-processes that are always performed in the same way, tasks that don't require "business knowledge" to perform, and system actions that can be programmed procedurally. Also, statements that are typically not business rules include procedural algorithms, database searches, and business or system events.

Guidelines for the Business Rule Acquisition Phase

The business rule acquisition phase is the most time-consuming, but it is a very important part of a business rules project. An experienced business rules analyst using a structured methodology seeks quality rules and traces them to the business goals and objectives. The job of documenting business processes at a detailed level will naturally expose the parts of the process in which rules are used.

Where and How to Find the Business Rules

The business rule analyst seeks a variety of knowledgeable rule sources such as human experts, policy and procedures documents, data models, object models, training guidelines, legacy code, and regulatory guidelines.

During the business rules acquisition phase, the business rule analyst extracts the rule statements (expressed in natural business language) and associates them to a specific part of the business process. In the business rule analysis phase, the analyst transforms these rule statements into more structured and detailed *condition-action* statements, as defined by the business rule architect. Often, a single rule statement will yield many *condition-action* statements. The rule design phase further transforms these statements into highly structured executable rules.

Business Rule Analysis Guidelines

The business rule analyst may find it helpful to group rules into sets; first, to help business people understand the rules in context, and second, to assist developers in determining how the business rules are best implemented and used in applications. Ideas for useful rule groupings are below.

1. Presentation rule sets, such as:

   Data collection: Identify missing required information.

   Simple field edits: Verify user input based on data available in memory.

   Complex field edits: Verify user input based on data available in memory and related data in permanent storage; determine which related data needs to be accessed.

2. Business process rule sets, such as:

   Attribute testing: Determine valid and required attributes for business procedures, policies and guidelines.

   Threshold testing: Compare data values to high and low thresholds.

3. Algorithmic rule sets, such as:

   Reference data: Table values represented as individual rules.

   Calculations: Complex computations and algorithms.

Business Rule Implementation Guidelines

The implementation decision for business rules should focus on how the rules are to be used and who is going to use them. Otherwise, the business rules may be lost and mismanaged if this decision is not made appropriately.

Today's applications have a choice of implementing business rules in many ways, including in a BRMS, BPMS (business process management system), business objects, databases, software packages, or custom-developed code.

Determining whether a group of rules should be represented in a database or a rule base is often not easy to decide. The following guidelines might help developers make this decision:

If more than about 10 repetitive rules are required to validate the storing of information, the valid values may be easier to maintain if placed in an external database table. For example, if there is a relationship between each state and certain features of a product, it may be better to represent those relationships as a database table. If some rules involve testing data against thresholds, it may be better to represent the thresholds in a set of rules in a rule base.

Guidelines for Defining an Enterprise Business Rules Architecture

It takes an experienced business rules architect to structure the business rules in a way the business user understands. The business rules architecture focuses on the business goals and objectives rather than the technology goals and objectives. A well-defined business rules architecture communicates the business strategies to the IT resourses.

Guiding Principles for Defining an Enterprise Business Rules Architecture

The following guidelines may assist a business rule architect in the development of a business rules architecture:

- Capture an expression of the business rules that is understandable, maintainable, and usable to the business user.

- Formalize and organize the business rules and rule sets (rule bases) in a logical structure, and make that structure available to the business community enterprise wide, and to the business analyst who will populate them.

- Follow standard naming conventions for business rules and business terms.

- Architect rule bases to minimize performance bottlenecks.

- Define the implementation strategies and tools as a joint effort between the business rules architect and technology architect.

- Select technology and tools that best support the rules behind the business problem, and allow business users to handle their core knowledge to make better decisions, where possible.

- Use a structured methodology and establish metrics for measuring the quality of the business process and rules.

Business Rules Design Guidelines

Below are tips for the rule architects and rule analysts for designing rule bases

- Design rule flow to follow the related use case sequence or to navigate business product conditions.

- Use rule flow to sequence the maintenance and testing of rule sets.

- Define a structure to group and package the rules into smaller rule sets for optimum performance.

- Parameterize rules coupled with database tables for repetitive table and value set processing.

- Structure decision tables to keep the business rules concise, and ensure outer conditions do not result in significant duplication of data to avoid performance penalties.

- Organize rules to allow expansion and specialization by business functions like insurance products.

- Focus first on core rules to set the default standard for similar rules. Specialized rules will then become customized instances of the core rules, such as by state and industry class.

- Include for all rules the effective date, and manage versions of rule sets for various effective time periods.

Roles and Responsibilities of Individuals Involved in Business Rules Architecture

This section provides an idea of the type of technical roles needed for a business rules project and how they interact with other project teams.

For organizations aiming for delivering enterprise business rules applications (RMM Level 3), consider establishing a **Business Rules Center of Excellence.** A Business Rules Center of Excellence plays a key role in promoting and establishing the Business Rules Approach and project concepts. This center can oversee all business rules projects and help coordinate and collaborate with technology teams and business groups. To head the group, a business rules project champion who has the experience in multiple projects and has captured the best practices is of great value.

The following are the technical roles and responsibilities needed for business rules projects.

1. Business Rules Architect
2. Business Rule Analyst
3. Systems Integration Engineer

The Business Rules Architect

The Business Rules Architect is a new role that combines knowledge of process and rules and business object model. The role of a Business Rules Architect is to define the rule architecture, including rule object model and rule flow for the business rules component under development. This role is responsible for grouping related and segregating unrelated requirements, conceptualization of the business rule base architecture, and many other architecture/design-related tasks. To perform this function, the Business Rule Architect interacts heavily with the business analysts acting as domain experts in the business requirements for the application under development.

The design responsibilities of the Business Rules Architect include, but are not limited to, the following:

- Lead a series of business requirements analysis sessions, in concert with the business analyst, through which the business requirements for the software application under development are to be identified.

- Design and architect a business rule solution for the implementation of those business requirements, which includes definition of rule sets and rule templates.

- Design and specify implementation architectures for all business rules within the software application under development.

- Supervise and direct the development of business rules and/or rule bases that implement the business requirements described above.

The Business Rules Architect must have competence and experience in object-oriented analysis (OOA), modeling, and all other aspects of the analysis and design of an application's object models. He/she must be able to design a business object model that is intuitive to business analysts, yet effectively represents the business data and processes of the application.

Business Rules Analyst

The Business Rules Analyst's core competency is in the domain of the business policies to be represented in the business rules of the application. This role is responsible for extracting, documenting, and analyzing all business rules for an application. This position can be filled by a competent Business Analyst who has been formally trained in harvesting and analyzing business rules and business rule management technologies. This role works with the Business Process and Rules Architect and Systems Integration Engineer during the requirements and design phases. This can sometimes be combined with a heads-down development role with an additional focus on generating the technical rules for the application under development. This role may also be responsible for rules implementation and testing. The direction today, however, is often to separate the analysis role from the technical development role.

Systems Integration Engineer

This individual is responsible for contributing to, and implementing, all of the designs specified by the Business Rules Architect. These responsibilities include implementing all interfaces to rules-based components, the business object model, and infrastructure components of the business rule bases.

The Controversy of Who Owns the Business Rules

To be politically correct, the corporation or government agency itself legally owns the business rules that guide it. The question here is who, within the organization, is empowered to steward those rules through their changes on behalf of the legal organization.

There is always confusion in organizations as to who should have such power over business rules (and business processes and business data). However, in a business-driven methodology for business rules, a company's operations management drives the business rules projects. The operations management stewards rule changes because the business rules are focused on the objectives and the goals set by the business.

Unfortunately, more often than not, the stewarding business operations area does not have the organizational structure or resources to accommodate the business process and rule analysis functions. In such cases, IT resources do so. Even so, the senior business executives and operations managers need to review their current organizational structure and position themselves to manage and steward the core business knowledge from a high level.

A well-trained business rules analyst who is a domain expert may be appropriate to steward the business rules and business process on a project-by-project basis on behalf of the true business stewards.

Summary

The success of a business rules project is based on a comprehensive understanding of the business. The interrelationship of the business goals, objectives, metrics, organization structure, business processes, and decisions is crucial knowledge to many business initiatives. Business rules are simply another aspect of business knowledge that now emerges as needing greater integration and attention, and to be available to the business community.

A better understanding of the business rules and business requirements also helps the technical communities develop better systems requirements and prevent scope creep.

Using a structured methodology helps define metrics for the quality of the business rules and business process. Also, it reinforces the traceability of business rules to the business goals and objectives.

The most important points in this chapter are:

- Business rules should no longer be buried in business and systems requirements.

- The business rule acquisition phase is important, and is usually led by a business rule analyst.

- An enterprise business rules architecture is structured by a business rules architect, who establishes standards for and organization of rule sets, while also assisting with technology selection.

- Business rules can be implemented in various ways, usually determined by a business rule architect or analyst.

- A Business Rules Center of Excellence is helpful in establishing and promoting a standard Business Rules Approach and technology.

- Proper stewardship of business rules belongs with the business management, but is often facilitated by IT analysts, due to a shortage of business resources.

Positioning the Enterprise for Business Rules: People, Processes, and Organization

Brian Stucky

The use of Business Rule Management Systems (BRMS) is growing at a rapid rate. Industry analysts predict a significant increase in the quantity of business processes and applications built with the Business Rules Approach. As these applications proliferate, it will be essential to provide stewardship and governance to support intelligent and consistent use of the technology. This is particularly true for those organizations that wish to embrace the Business Rules Approach and support multiple business-driven projects, both individually and at an enterprise level.

While the promise of BRMS is alluring, realizing the benefits requires more than finding rules and integrating a business rule engine. The people responsible for managing rules, the processes required to ensure safe and consistent application and management of rules, and the organization that desires to utilize rules as a true corporate asset must all be positioned correctly.

Modern BRMS promise collaboration as a means to allow business and technical resources to communicate more easily. BRMS vendors often suggest that business users will be able to take over many of the tasks previously dedicated to technical resources. While the vendors now offer tools that bring these promises closer to fruition, we are on the cusp of a business rule revolution where a new resource—the business rule analyst—will play a critical role in the enterprise.

These same business rule analysts will be responsible for rule stewardship. In the simplest sense, stewardship deals with the standards and processes required to guide, monitor, and control business rules and all supporting material through their life cycle. Specific roles and associated capabilities must be designed to ensure business rule correctness, consistency, and traceability. Pulling these roles together necessitates a new level of collaboration among resources at many levels.

Finally, at the enterprise level, we need governance processes that emphasize the consistency and quality of rules when viewed as a true corporate asset—how they are positioned to enable reuse across the enterprise. This governance must guarantee that activities surrounding business rules during their life cycle are tied closely to the standards and operational models that already exist within an organization.

This chapter delineates the critical points across these three areas—people, process, and organization—that must be considered when an enterprise wishes to move to the Business Rules Approach. Therefore, the chapter covers:

- The call for business rules
- The starting point for business rules in the enterprise
- People: The collaborative organization
- Process: Stewardship for the tactical organization
- Organization: Governance for the strategic organization
- Summary
- Key points

The Call for Business Rules

The benefits that are realized by moving to the Business Rules Approach have been discussed frequently. The notion of an *agile* enterprise, capable of rapid change and continuous improvement of services, is appealing on many levels. The ability to handle rapid change facilitates both a quick reaction to dynamic market conditions and proactive launching of programs to achieve or maintain a competitive edge. However, this move to a zero time-to-market is only the tip of the iceberg in terms of the potential benefits brought by business rules.

Implicit benefits will be realized by the mere act of going through the rigor of knowing all the rules and creating a complete and accurate list of them. This alone can pay huge dividends for an organization. The same rules often exist in multiple places, are managed independently, and are frequently not synchronized. This exercise of rule harvesting, elicitation, documentation, and analysis is a critical step towards enabling consistency across systems in the enterprise.

More explicit benefits are possible because BRMS software has become more sophisticated. Facilities exist now so that business analysts can be empowered to write, manage and deploy business rules with little to no technical intervention. With this capability, an enterprise is able to support a true business-driven need for change. Now the individuals who have traditionally been responsible for understanding the business can bring their expertise directly into production systems.

Ultimately we would like to view business rules as a true corporate asset—a valuable resource, accessible to all, that may be viewed as a common form of communication. This truly collaborative platform can then be the springboard to a wealth of opportunities:

- Faster time-to-market

- Simulation of various scenarios before implementation

- Flexible and responsive reaction to customer needs

- Increased ability to meet compliance and regulatory demands

The advantages of the Business Rules Approach are overwhelming. Software available to implement a BRMS has made tremendous gains over the last decade. Success stories are becoming more frequent. However, if nothing else, this chapter should be viewed as a cautionary tale. Despite this great promise, the full advantages of business rules will not be reached simply by purchasing software and setting about the task of finding the rules. There are a number of areas that must be clearly understood and carefully considered when attempting to bring rules to the enterprise.

The Starting Point for Business Rules in the Enterprise

Any discussion of preparing for rules must begin with the most important asset of an organization: the people. BRMS software is touted as the ultimate in enabling collaboration and providing a common platform through which all resources (business, technical, and management) may communicate. However, the need for people with a new set of skills is often overlooked. Finding, articulating, documenting, analyzing, implementing, testing, managing, and deploying rules necessitates people who are a little of everything—business analyst, technician, and manager. Only with these individuals in place will an enterprise become a truly *collaborative* organization.

Stewardship of rules is a topic of increasing interest but the term is still used somewhat broadly. It can best be viewed as the responsibility for taking good care of resources entrusted to one—the concept of "responsible caretaking." What does this mean for business rules? It should mean the creation of a technical, business, and management environment that can truly embrace rules as a means to support rapid solution development and maintenance. These encompass the tools and processes that must be in place so that an enterprise can safely, consistently, and accurately move towards an environment capable of rapid and immediate change. Only with these processes in place for projects employing business rules will the truly *tactical* organization be enabled.

The final piece of the positioning puzzle is the idea of business rule governance. At this level, we move up from the tactical project viewpoint to the governing view of the enterprise. Governance defines the model to ensure optimal reuse of services and enforcement of corporate policies. Ultimately these policies determine the long-term strategy and direction of an organization. Many organizations do not have the necessary infrastructure in place to support this need as it is best driven via a Center of Excellence or similar entity, variously called a Technology Center of Excellence or Business Rules Center of Excellence. Only with this overseeing body in place can the truly *strategic* enterprise be realized.

People: The Collaborative Organization

Organizations have traditionally cultivated a huge chasm between technical and business resources. Often, the only form of communication between the two is requirements, and they are rarely in a form that is desired by both sides. With the modern BRMS offering a vehicle through which both business and technical analysts can communicate, we must consider whether either resource alone is sufficient. The ideal new resource would simply combine technical and business expertise. While this individual does not need to be deeply technically oriented, he or she should be able to codify policy and express it logically in the forms of rules. While not strictly a business analyst, he or she must have a solid foundation in the business domain and be able to grasp business concepts. Business skills are more important, especially as the constantly evolving and improving BRMS provides more of the necessary technical features. However, the mix of business and technical skills is still critically important to attain long-term business rule management success.

It is fairly easy to look at an individual placed in the new role of a business rule analyst and determine whether or not he or she is up to the task. It is not so easy to describe a set of characteristics that will guarantee selecting the right candidate. As the adoption of business rules spreads, we will likely see more specialized individuals trained and well-versed in the art of business rules. For now, consider the traits that would suggest someone has the potential to fill this role.

The business rule analyst will be responsible for handling rules throughout the business rule life cycle. This means the business rule analyst will identify, harvest, document, analyze, implement, test, manage, and deploy rules. Consequently, he or she must first and foremost have a strong business or domain background. This is probably more important than having a deep technical skill set. If an organization's policy cannot be correctly interpreted, then implementation via business rules will not provide benefits. Technical skills are most important in terms of logical analysis—taking policy and expressing it formally so the correct decisions can be reached. A business rule analyst must have strong communication skills, as he or she and the BRMS will actually serve as the collaboration platform that brings business, technical and management resources together. Finally, the business rule analyst must be able to pay close attention to small details while keeping the big picture in mind. Small enhancements that may seem to bring about a performance or clarity improvement are of little value if they result in losing sight of the primary goals.

Process: Stewardship for the Tactical Organization

The enterprise that is able to approach zero time-to-market with business rules will have done so by acknowledging the need to create processes to enable stewardship. The areas discussed in this section are not presented as a *how* but rather as a *what*. These are the areas that must each be explored and considered. The final look and feel of each may vary from organization to organization, but they must be addressed in some fashion.

Development with business rules is inherently an iterative process. As simple as that statement may seem, it can cause difficulties when this does not comply with the traditional means of development at an organization. However, it is critical to acknowledge this characteristic and adapt accordingly. Rules will move continually through a process of discovery, analysis, implementation, testing, and validation or deployment. Moving through this cycle with a rule or rule set will invariably result in restarting the process for other rules. This happens both through initial development and ultimately in a maintenance mode.

Like other software, business rules have a life cycle that usually varies from one organization to another. Defining and maintaining rules with respect to this life cycle is critically important. Business rule analyst roles may be created that pertain to various stages in the life cycle. Security may differ across different points in the life cycle. The life cycle can be created with respect to the state of a rule (draft, integrated testing, user acceptance testing, and deployment) or a path very specific to the domain in which they are created.

Rapid change and deployment via business rules is certainly powerful. However, this can place a huge burden on an organization's change management processes if frequent rule changes are not handled properly. Although speed is clearly a tremendous benefit, it is imperative to strike a balance between speed and control. Fast change that is uncontrolled and potentially sloppy can result in extremely dire consequences. In large part, how this is handled will depend on the enterprise architecture paths that are already in place. Rules may be viewed as either code (they influence the logic of program processing), or data (they are often persisted in a database and can be viewed as the data required by a business rule engine). It is important for an organization to decide whether to manage rules as code or as data, simply because the change management processes for code tends not to be the same as that for data. Regardless of the path, processes for versioning, metadata, persistence, deployment, security and testing must all be established.

Testing is sometimes overlooked in terms of its criticality in the business rule process. If rules are to be deployed rapidly, and if business rule analysts are to make these changes, it becomes even more important to establish complete testing procedures to maintain the integrity of the ultimate production system. At a high level, testing should allow managers and business rule analysts to ensure that rules being created or modified are, in fact, consistent with the policy they represent. We can view testing at four different levels:

- Syntactic: to ensure a well-formed rule that is readable by the system (most software has this level of testing already built in)

- Semantic: to ensure a specific rule behaves as desired

- End-to-end: to ensure the rule still functions properly when viewed in the larger context of a rule set or rule service

- Simulation: to analyze the results of a policy change and predict the impact on business.

While testing is a common and well-understood process for the technician, this is not necessarily the case for the business or business rule analyst. The facilities created must be intuitive and comprehensive, and may include regression test suites, measures of expected results, and tools that can assist in the analysis and understanding of errors that are detected.

Organization: Governance for the Strategic Organization

Adoption of business rules over the past decade was often limited to individual projects within an organization. In many cases, other areas of the same company ventured down the business rule road and ended up with a completely different methodology for applying business rules—and in some cases with a different, potentially duplicated BRMS! However, the latest generation of software has been constructed with the enterprise view in mind. Consequently, more organizations are taking a global view when considering business rules. This can be extremely useful when addressing business rule governance.

Rule governance refers to the standards and processes needed to guide and monitor business rules and all relevant artifacts through their life cycle. It is here that we can begin to consider rules as a true corporate asset as they will be integrated within the standards and operational models that already exist in an organization, and can then be partitioned to enable reuse across the enterprise.

Rule governance, especially across automated systems, can best be administered by the creation of a Technology Center of Excellence. This same model may be used for various technology approaches (e.g., business process management or business intelligence). The idea is the same: to provide technology governance in alignment with the strategic direction of the enterprise. Although the title seems to focus on technology, these groups in the new enterprise must increase business involvement to align technology capabilities with the strategic direction of the business. This group must be the focal point that serves as a clearinghouse for information that links people, processes, and the technology itself. Ultimately this group should encourage adoption and intelligent use of the technology.

A Business Rules Center of Excellence must clearly be a cross-disciplinary group that embraces both technology and business viewpoints. Perhaps no other technology purports to bring these two sides together as closely as business rules. To that end, both sides must provide input to support intelligent and consistent use across the enterprise. A charter for this group might include the following:

- Define the appropriate use of rules technology: when and where it should be used

- Understand and articulate the business value of a rule implementation

- Define rule conventions, standards, and best practices

- Understand and encourage rule reuse

- Provide outreach and communication, internal and external

The group may be staffed in a variety of ways, but should include executive level sponsors representing both business and technical interests, a group lead, leads from various areas including operations, architecture, staffing, and change management, and diverse members from across the enterprise. Filling several key roles can make the group more successful. The *Advocate* should be an executive with high visibility in the enterprise. Ideally, this executive will be from a business area or other non-technical division. The *Evangelist* should be the group lead that becomes the face of business rules within the organization. This person will be primarily responsible for outreach and communication to spread the word of business rules as often as possible. The *Scientist* is usually someone who serves as an enterprise architect and can guarantee adherence to corporate standards and guidelines as business rules are integrated. The *Visionary* will continually look ahead for new methods, domains, and applications where the technology may be applied. Finally, no group is successful without enthusiastic members that both provide important input to the group and become disciples to take the message across the enterprise.

Summary

The adoption of BRMS is rapidly becoming a core component of the advanced enterprise. The technology is well beyond the early adopter phase at this point and is close to becoming a standard component in the corporate technology infrastructure. As the technology, methodology and software continues to mature, the case for enterprise adoption grows even stronger. The decision to move to the Business Rules Approach will no longer be made by technologists on a project, but instead by executives desirous of fully utilizing business rules as a true corporate asset. This is, after all, what the Business Rule Revolution is truly about.

The great promise of business rules does not come without potential pitfalls. The wise enterprise will analyze and develop a solid foundation of people, processes, and organization in order to become the collaborative, tactical and strategic, that can be realized with the integration of business rules.

Key Points

- BRMSs are becoming more mainstream.

- Business rules are key to creating an agile enterprise.

- Simply deciding to embrace business rules and purchasing business rule management software is not enough to guarantee success.

- New resource types and people skills are necessary to create a truly collaborative environment.

- Processes must be established for business rule stewardship to enable a tactical enterprise.

- The organization must create governance for business rules to facilitate the strategic enterprise.

12 Achieving Rule Maturity for Competitive Advantage — A Case Study of Equifax

Linda Nieporent

Introduction

Equifax is a 107-year old global information solutions company that adopted the Business Rules Approach long before it was called "the Business Rules Approach." This industry leader implemented business policies in code before the Rete algorithm was designed by Charles Forgy, and separated out business policies into requirements documents well before the Business Rules Group formulated standards around business rules and their relationship with systems. Today, Equifax enables and secures global commerce through the data and services it provides for companies spanning a wide range of industries, including financial services, retail, healthcare, telecommunications/utilities, brokerage, insurance and government.

The systems that Equifax has built to support its core business depend heavily on business rules that enforce business policies. Equifax products are designed to help customers make informed decisions using the data it gathers and manages. Some of those decisions are internally driven by Equifax policies, but many are dictated by external customers. A given customer makes a request to Equifax for a credit report and for decisions on a set of questions, based on criteria set by the client. For decades, Equifax has separated out business rules from other aspects of its systems, both in requirements and in implementation, to help manage the complexity of the number of rules and the distributed nature of rule ownership. Initially, this was done on mainframe and mid-range systems in which Equifax managed rule separation by modularizing code. The next generation was *Decision Power*, a client/server system in which Equifax incorporated a home-grown rule engine, which did not allow business user authoring of rules.

The most recent advance is Equifax *InterConnect*, a credit decisioning platform based on a J2EE architecture and ILOG's JRules business rule management system (BRMS). *InterConnect* is a hosted service that Equifax customers access to view, modify, test and deploy the business rules that help them determine when to offer credit, how much credit to offer and which credit risks to avoid.

With *InterConnect*, Equifax is further recognizing the benefits of a business rules approach and business rules technology. *InterConnect* was inspired by increasing demands from customers for better support for their complex and frequently changing business rules. Customers were interested in viewing and changing their own rules as needed. In addition, customers needed the ability to manage change by introducing governance processes and ensuring that rule authors understand the business implications of rule changes.

This chapter discusses the following:
- A recent history of business rules at Equifax
- Why did Equifax select ILOG JRules?
- How is JRules helping Equifax?
- How have customer experiences like Equifax's influenced ILOG to enhance JRules?
- Lessons learned
- What do Equifax customers think?
- Looking ahead—*InterConnect* and JRules 6
- Summary
- References

A Recent History of Business Rules at Equifax

The business of credit has changed significantly over the last 20 to 30 years. Until the late 1980's, the credit reporting business was all about gathering data to build a credit history on consumers based on their payment history and information on loans, credit card accounts and other financial obligations. The use of this data was left to the judgment of individuals at banks, department stores and other businesses to determine the credit risk of a consumer. The evolution of credit scoring in the mid- to late 1980's shifted the emphasis from raw data on a credit report to an integrated interpretation of the data. Scoring provides an overall understanding of the individual's credit worthiness and takes into account, among other factors, the relative weight placed upon various aspects of the report.

Even with the introduction of scoring, utilization of credit reports was typically a simple system-to-system request for a credit report. In response, the entire report was provided to the requestor with no additional intelligence about the relevance of any particular information in the report. This practice led to increased demand for utilizing credit report data to make decisions that could help institutions manage risk while increasing revenue opportunities. Equifax worked with customers to develop batch processes that applied a set of business rules to sets of available consumer credit histories to determine lists of consumers to whom they would want to solicit business. This batch process was useful, but customers were soon clamoring for more timely solutions. Equifax launched *Decision Power* in the early 1990's to help customers take advantage of opportunities in cross-selling services to their consumers while they were involved in live interactions with the consumers. Initially, the goal was simply to take existing offline batch processing business rules and make the decision-making capability available in real time on an individual transaction basis. When an individual was opening a bank account, the bank could request a quick—and reliable—decision on whether, and on what terms, to offer a credit card account or a line of credit.

Decision Power

Decision Power was innovative in that it provided more than just the credit report; it also delivered a response consistent with the requestor's credit policy, e.g. "Approve the offer with a $2,000 credit limit" or "No, we have to deny the loan request because of x, y and z." This resulted in a significant change in the business of managing credit—from a time-consuming process requiring individual judgment to an immediate and consistent result with a built-in explanation. For example, creditors interested in tapping the sub-prime lending market require more intricate logic, utilizing data from a broader set of sources. In sub-prime lending it is critical to manage risk appropriately. Many consumers that were previously unable to secure credit were now able to do so, because creditors could distinguish more effectively among higher risk consumers.

As Equifax customers started to use *Decision Power*, greater opportunities became apparent. They developed more complex business rules to make finer distinctions among potential borrowers and identified more situations in which policies could be automated. They could expand from relatively easy credit decisions to more complex ones, increasing revenue opportunities within manageable risk guidelines. *Decision Power* was a client/server based system in which the business rules were hard-coded. The rules were separated from the other program code, enabling relatively quick modifications without integration concerns, but changes still required Equifax IT intervention. As customers became more sophisticated in their ongoing business rule requirements, Equifax needed a new platform on which to support them—and *InterConnect* was born.

InterConnect | Having moved beyond basic separation of business rules in specification documents and in program code, Equifax identified the need for a business rule management system as a core component of its new platform. Equifax needed a system that enabled it to:

- Deploy business rule changes quickly and without system disruption.
- Give customers the power to edit business rules and make changes to rules as needed. This required exposing business rules in a business-friendly language that resources outside of the IT department could easily understand.
- Provide real-time responses at high-volume transaction loads.
- Easily integrate the decision making components of the *InterConnect* platform with other modules.

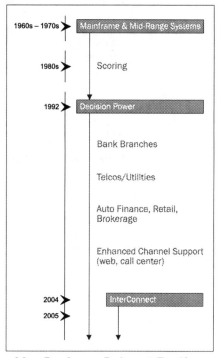

Figure 30: Business Rules at Equifax

Why did Equifax select ILOG JRules?

Once Equifax decided upon the incorporation of a business rule engine into its *InterConnect* platform, the company settled the "build vs. buy" question quickly, due to the availability of good commercial options and the inherent complexity of a rule engine. Because the rule engine would be a central and critical component of *InterConnect*, Equifax carefully considered the choice of vendor. Beyond the basic technical requirements, Equifax was seeking a relationship with a vendor who would work closely with them to ensure their success. In JRules, Equifax found a solid rule management platform with built-in flexibility and excellent performance. In ILOG, Equifax found a partner willing to work with them on extensions and customizations as needed and willing to listen to ongoing requirements as Equifax's own solution matured. Today, Equifax and ILOG continue to share product roadmaps to ensure they align as much as possible.

"Whenever we had a problem or needed a feature/function, ILOG was very accommodating and worked with us to ensure our success."

Fred Hughes, SVP Strategic Development, Equifax

How is JRules helping Equifax?

Equifax depends on several key features of ILOG JRules in the *InterConnect* platform.

High Performance Rule Engine and Rule Execution Server (RES)

Equifax considered performance an important criterion when selecting a BRMS. Equifax customers expect an average response time of no more than three seconds for execution. As an application service provider (ASP), Equifax expects to be able to handle 50,000 transactions per hour, with a reasonable infrastructure. Starting with its latest *InterConnect* release on JRules 5.1, Equifax takes advantage of Rule Execution Server (RES), which provides managed deployment with enhanced ruleset management, J2EE role-based security, and cluster management.

Business User Rule Management

Equifax's business users are not Equifax employees, but rather employees of Equifax customers. As an ASP, Equifax manages the core environment, development and maintenance of customer systems, with business rule maintenance performed by the customers themselves. During the initial setup of a customer implementation, an Equifax project team works with the customer to identify the necessary data sources, capture and implement the initial set of rules, and train customer personnel on using the system, including business rule maintenance.

Equifax uses the JRules Web Rule Editor as the interface for its business customers. As Equifax migrates *InterConnect* to JRules 6, this interface will be replaced by JRules Rule Team Server, providing a rule authoring environment designed specifically for business users in a friendly web-based application. Rule Team Server provides enhanced repository support with role-based permissions on a relational database repository, history tracking, baselining and rollback, and productivity tools such as queries and smart views.

Different customers place different demands on the rule maintenance environment—some change rules weekly, some monthly; some plan their changes well in advance, while others need to react more quickly to business pressures. What is universally important is that they can change the rules themselves, on their own schedules, and in a way that isn't disruptive to the overall application.

Making significant changes to business rules generally takes time, as customers must first become confident with rule management. At first, they will likely focus on simple changes such as adjusting acceptable score thresholds. As they grow more comfortable with such changes and become more confident with the tools, they will start to make more complex changes, such as adding and removing conditions or adding entirely new business rules.

"Our clients' first implementations have become trivial; customers are becoming more and more comfortable with complex rules involving multiple data sources and they can more confidently make decisions on riskier consumers."

Sandeep Gupta, VP B2B Software Development, Equifax

Flexibility in Rule Language and Artifacts

Flexibility was also a critical factor in Equifax's selection of JRules. Working with ILOG JRules 4.x and 5.x, Equifax has customized the user interface for customers in several ways. Some customizations are to assist in the initial project startup phase and others are for ongoing rule maintenance by business users. Since Equifax provides much of the data used by each customer, they have pre-built business object models (BOMs) representing common data sources. They use plug-ins to import and merge the BOMs required for a given project, along with any specific data sources the customer is introducing, to set up the rule authoring environment. They also make available a set of starter tasks, such as "Pull Equifax credit report," that are commonly used but can be modified, to speed the model build process. Since many of the variables used in business rules are also common, and can require complex definitions, Equifax has incorporated a mechanism to re-use variable definitions across business rules. To expand upon the types of rules that can be captured and managed, they have created a custom business rule language, incorporating their own proprietary grammar for certain rule types, using the JRules Business Rule Language Definition Framework (BRLDF). For developer testing, they have integrated JUnit testing into the Rule Builder (the developers' rule authoring environment).

How Have Customer Experiences Like Equifax's Influenced ILOG to Enhance JRules?

ILOG is constantly seeking feedback from customers on how to improve its products, and many of these enhancements are evident in ILOG JRules 6. Although Equifax tends to be a "power user" of ILOG JRules BRMS technology, they share requirements with many ILOG customers. In continuing to strengthen a BRMS from the base of a rule engine and basic rule editing facilities, ILOG has established four foundational capabilities for its BRMS products:

- Full empowerment for business teams

- Full productivity for technical teams

- Synchronized full life-cycle business rule management

- Unequalled performance

Full empowerment for business teams means that business users can:

- Satisfy regulatory and business imperatives for security, traceability and auditability of policy changes

- Learn business rule management quickly

- Author, maintain, and deploy business rules directly, safely, and confidently

Full productivity for technical teams means that developers and architects can:

- Apply corporate development standards, best practices, and processes to applications that incorporate business rules

- Master business rule management quickly, working with familiar techniques

- Integrate BRMS naturally and natively within current and future technical infrastructures

Synchronized full life-cycle business rule management enables both teams to:

- Work on several release cycles simultaneously, maintaining the release in production while preparing the next minor release and the next major release

- Share and reuse rules among rule authors with different professional backgrounds and languages

- Ensure confidence and control over the rule management life cycle

Lessons Learned

With *InterConnect*'s second major release due out in 2006, and more customers moving to the platform each quarter, Equifax shared some "lessons learned" with ILOG that could help others embarking on building business rules systems.

- **Keep the system flexible:** Equifax credits much of *InterConnect*'s success as well as its ability to plan for major product enhancements to a flexible approach to business rule management. ILOG JRules is designed precisely for such flexibility, but make sure that the other components are integrated in a way that doesn't obstruct the natural flexibility of a rules-based approach.

- **Employ good governance:** Good governance over business rule change must not be overlooked. This is critical whether the people changing the business rules are within the company or in an external organization, such as is the case with Equifax systems. For a typical Equifax customer, a small mistake in a rule change could have significant financial implications. While you want to keep the governance process agile to ensure changes can be quickly accommodated, don't skimp on the approval process.

- **Provide testing and simulation tools:** Testing and simulation are critical to business user confidence in exercising control over production business rules. Business users themselves are often the driving force behind putting business rule changes in the hands of policy makers. However, once given that power, many are skittish about implementing changes that could have negative side effects. Once they become comfortable making such changes, the natural evolution is to work on how they can make their rules better. Using historical data and simulation capability, business users can perform what-if analysis on potential rule changes and improve the rulesets they deploy. Incorporating a testing and simulation module into *InterConnect* became an important priority for the second major release of the platform.

- **Know your data:** At Equifax, one impact of exposing business users more directly to business rules and enabling them to change them has been an explosion of data sources used. One of the ways in which business customers expand and increase the complexity of their business rules is to utilize data from additional sources. This requires careful management of the overall set of data, organized into one or more BOMs that are the basis for the business rules written.

- **When investigating technology, think broadly:** As you mature in the discipline of business rules, your technology needs will move beyond basic rule authoring and a business rule engine to a broader Business Rule Management System, with an emphasis on longer-term rule management, business user tooling and testing and simulation capabilities.

- **Pay attention to processes for development and deployment:** Due to the nature of BRMS technology, particularly the intended redeployment of business rules as they change, processes for development, deployment and change management may need to be revised.

- **Train your people and utilize expert resources as needed:** This applies both to the IT resources involved in the initial development of the system and to those people who will be involved in maintaining the system on an operational basis. Operational teams should be involved from the beginning of the development process. Equifax focused mainly on ensuring its internal resources gained the skills needed to build and maintain the system but also worked with ILOG professional services to ensure that key pieces were done optimally. Finally, do not forget the business analysts and business people who will be involved in designing and maintaining the system.

What do Equifax Customers Think?

Equifax customers are the true end users of the *InterConnect* system. The benefits to banks, credit card issuers and telecommunications companies that rely on *InterConnect* to make decisions about what they can and should offer to prospective (and existing) consumers are substantial. The speed with which a customer can be initially set up on the system, due to the core infrastructure in place and an established and repeatable process of gathering customer-specific requirements, makes the solution a compelling choice. The ongoing ability to modify the business rules used to deliver results to the customers is a significant competitive advantage for Equifax. Once customers are exposed to the capabilities the rule-driven system offers, they gain a world of new opportunities.

> "Providing our bankers with tools that help them make more informed credit decisions is critical to helping us provide world standard service to our clients and manage risk. InterConnect, Equifax's business rules management system, gives us a powerful solution that fits well with our front-end system, custom models and SBFE interface."
>
> **Carlos Goodrick, Senior Vice President and SBB Risk Manager, BB&T Small Business Banking**

Looking Ahead— *InterConnect* and JRules 6

At its core, the Business Rules Approach is about bringing business and IT groups together—aligning goals, enabling collaboration and producing a better result by focusing on business user-defined business logic. That logic is implemented in systems that, by their nature, are maintainable with continued business/IT collaboration. JRules 6 embodies the spirit of this approach. Each new module of JRules 6—Rule Studio, Rule Team Server, Rule Execution Server, and Rule Scenario Manager—offers additional value to Equifax above and beyond that already realized with previous versions of JRules.

Rule Team Server is a highly scalable rule management server and repository with a collaborative web environment for authoring, managing, validating and deploying business rules. Rule Team Server provides enterprise-class content management for rules.

- Rule Team Server's (RTS) core business user focused capabilities, plus customizable look and feel and extension points, will allow Equifax to use RTS as the public face of *InterConnect*.

- Business rule management capabilities (versioning, baseline management, role-based permissions) of Rule Team Server will enhance Equifax customers' ability to successfully manage their rule changes.

Rule Scenario Manager delivers powerful ruleset testing and business simulation capabilities. Rule Scenario Manager provides an integrated environment for verifying the correctness of rules and simulating changes in business policies. Customizable, it can be tailored to enterprise data stores, deployment processes, and reporting requirements.

- Equifax is investigating how best to incorporate Rule Scenario Manager into *InterConnect* to provide further capabilities to end users for testing and simulation.

Rule Studio is an integrated development environment (IDE) for rule applications. Rule Studio fits directly into the Eclipse family of IDEs, which includes the Eclipse IDE, IBM Rational Application Developer and IBM Rational Software Architect, BEA Workshop, and others. Rule Studio supports ruleset debugging and deployment to ILOG JRules Rule Execution Server, and enables collaboration among business rule authors through Rule Team Server. Benefits to Equifax include:

- Management of multiple/composite BOMs, particularly important to an ASP solution such as InterConnect, is made much easier.

- Establishing dependencies among projects to create composite projects that share existing components (BOMs, rulesets, templates, etc.) provides needed flexibility in designing applications. Equifax can more easily segment projects by customer while maintaining common BOM information and templates for all customers.

- The move to the Eclipse platform provides automatic integration with JUnit as well as other Eclipse-based functionality such as source code control systems.

- And for continued individual or forward-thinking extensions, developers can take advantage of the Eclipse plug-in framework combined with ILOG JRules's inherent flexibility.

Rule Execution Server is a robust J2SE- and J2EE-compliant managed rule execution environment. Rule Execution Server is used to deploy business rule SOA services to the leading web and application servers from IBM, BEA, JBoss, Oracle and Apache. Rule Execution Server includes a web administration console and components for synchronous, asynchronous and web service-based invocation of business rules. Rule Execution Server is fully integrated with Rule Studio and Rule Team Server to support business rule deployment for both developers and policy managers.

- As an application service provider, the reliability and ease of administration in Rule Execution Server solidify Equifax's confidence in ILOG JRules as an integral component of *InterConnect*.

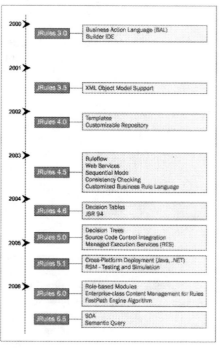

Figure 31: Major features of JRules by release

Summary

- Equifax's journey to fulfilling the full promise of a Business Rules Approach has been a long one.

- Success has been found along the way, increasing over time to create a flexible and efficient IT infrastructure and a platform that provides enormous business value to Equifax and its customers.

  - Initial separation of business rules from other specifications and code enabled Equifax to respond to customer demand for changes relatively quickly.

  - Further separation with *Decision Power* and improved technology enabled real-time responsiveness with automated decisions.

  - *InterConnect* leverages a full BRMS to empower business users and facilitate enhanced back-end processing.

- At this stage, Equifax has the tools and the business experience to focus on maximizing business value by:

  - Putting more rule authoring and management in the control of policy managers.

  - Enabling policy managers to create the best rulesets through testing and simulation.

  - Managing a smoothly running, high performance execution environment.

- The capabilities Equifax can offer with ILOG JRules at the heart of its *InterConnect* platform have changed the way its customers do business

  - Better decision-making capabilities enable creditors to increase their customer touch points and the types of products they can offer.

- Effectively managing business decisions through rapid deployment of business rules provides creditors the ability to take advantage of new business opportunities as they arise.

- Repository and administrative tools help Equifax and its customers manage change and complexity, freeing them to focus on the content of business rules more than the processes used to manage them.

References

Moore, Ariana-Michele. "Business Rule Management Systems and Financial Services: Equifax as a Case Study." Celent Communications, 2005. http://www.celent.com.

About Equifax (www.equifax.com)
Equifax Inc. is a global leader in information technology that enables and secures global commerce with consumers and businesses. We are one of the largest sources of consumer and commercial data. Utilizing our databases, advanced analytics, and proprietary enabling technology, we provide real-time answers for our customers. This innovative ability to transform information into intelligence is valued by customers across a wide range of industries and markets. Headquartered in Atlanta, Georgia, Equifax employs approximately 4,600 people in 13 countries throughout North America, Latin America and Europe. Equifax was founded 107 years ago, and today is a member of Standard & Poor's (S&P) 500® Index. Our common stock is traded on the New York Stock Exchange under the symbol EFX.

About ILOG (www.ilog.com)
ILOG delivers software and services that empower customers to make better decisions faster and manage change and complexity. Over 2,500 global corporations and more than 465 leading software

vendors rely on ILOG's market-leading business rule management system (BRMS), optimization and visualization software components, to achieve dramatic returns on investment, create market-defining products and services, and sharpen their competitive edge. The BRMS market share leader, ILOG was founded in 1987 and employs more than 700 people worldwide.

Trademark notices:

ILOG, CPLEX and the ILOG logotype are registered trademarks, and all ILOG product names are trademarks of ILOG.

Equifax and Equifax *Decision Power* are registered trademarks, and *InterConnect* is a trademark of Equifax Inc.

All other brand, product, and company names are trademarks or registered trademarks of their respective holders.

The Blaze Advisor Business Rules Management System

The Blaze Advisor™ business rules management system (BRMS) from Fair Isaac Corporation is a complete solution for enterprise business rules management, involving rule service design, authoring, testing, service deployment, and maintenance. A rule service, or a decision service, can be defined as a monolithic view of all the conditions and actions that need to be considered in performing a self-contained, callable decisioning process as a service function from a larger application. In a service-oriented architecture (SOA), these decision services are common in the business service layer, as shown in Figure 32. They might be exposed from within legacy applications or developed as business services.

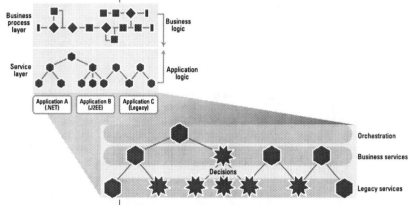

Figure 32: The Role of Decision Services in SOA

To create decision services, Blaze Advisor has a number of software components that interact with business applications and data. These components include an integrated development environment (IDE), generated rule management applications (light, web-based applications for editing business rules in a non-technical way), a rule repository, a rule server and engine, and SmartForms for Blaze Advisor. These components fit together to deliver a complete business rules management system as shown in Figure 33. It is important to understand the role of these components before explaining their use in an enterprise policy hub.

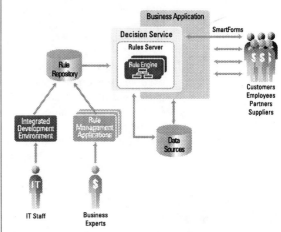

Figure 33: Overview of the Blaze Advisor Environment

1. **Integrated Development Environment (IDE)**
   Decision services are defined using Blaze Advisor's IDE. The IDE is a complete environment for decision service design, rule authoring, rule testing, creating rules management applications, and for specifying design templates for rules (covered in more detail later). The IDE also connects directly to enterprise or external data sources and web services to allow the rule service to use these when executing decisions. The IDE is available in six European and Asian languages.

2. **Rule Management Applications**
   Blaze Advisor rule management applications allow controlled rule editing and creation by non-technical users through standard web technologies. These template-driven applications expose some or all of the rules for

controlled editing by non-technical users. These rules can be changed in running systems directly or through a formal release process.

3. **Rule Repository**
   Business rules are maintained in a Blaze Advisor rule repository that provides the runtime service with the latest definitions of rules, as updated by the development environment and maintenance applications. The repository provides versioning and management services across all the components. The Blaze Advisor repository is common across all Blaze Advisor supported platforms (Java, .NET and COBOL).

4. **Rule Server and Engine**
   When an application asks Blaze Advisor to perform a decision service, it is executed using the Blaze Advisor Rule Server and Engine. The Rule Server manages scalability, multiple service requests, rule updates, and more. The Engine executes the rules with best-in-class performance. In addition the Engine can access necessary data sources or services to obtain information as and when needed to perform the service.

5. **SmartForms for Blaze Advisor**
   SmartForms for Blaze Advisor allows rule services to publish a web-form based GUI to collect data from a human user. The forms generated use a rules-based approach to collect and verify data, taking advantage of the X-Forms standard to deliver next-generation HTML forms and of AJAX to maximize responsiveness. The use of rules for guided data capture ensures that necessary data is captured and unnecessary data is not.

Key Strengths and Features of Blaze Advisor

Blaze Advisor is well-recognized as having the following strengths in the business rules marketplace:

- Extensive history and experience
- Heterogeneous environment support for Java, .NET and COBOL
- Powerful rule repository
- Top-of-the-line performance
- Extensive integration capability
- Patented rule management application generation
- Predictive analytic models

Extensive history and experience

Blaze Advisor today is the result of over 20 years of experience in developing a platform for expert systems and business rules management. The current product was built from the ground up 10 years ago and is now mature and stable. Not only does it have a consistent history of major and minor product releases over that time, Blaze Advisor is consistently the first product to introduce new innovations in the business rules marketplace and to embrace standards. For instance, Blaze Advisor was first to introduce the rule flow, decision tree and scorecard rule-entry metaphors. Blaze Advisor is widely used with over 500 customers worldwide and is, in addition, a platform for *all* other software application development at Fair Isaac.

Heterogeneous environment support for Java, .NET and COBOL

Blaze Advisor is unique in its ability to operate in today's heterogeneous environment. Not only is a complete rule development and maintenance environment available for both the .NET and Java environments, the execution of business rules is supported on .NET, Java Standard Edition, and Java Enterprise Edition as well as COBOL. The product also has a single syntax and common enterprise-class rule repository across all platforms, allowing business rules to be shared across all three deployment environments from a single repository.

Powerful rule repository

The repository itself supports, and ships with, best practices for developing a structured, management environment for business rules. Through the addition of management properties, it supports an extensible meta-model that can be customized by organizations to meet their unique needs and methodology. In addition, powerful queries and actions for repository reporting and management, along with release management, are provided directly from the IDE, making it practical to manage business rules across large enterprises.

Top-of-the-line performance

Top-of-the-line performance is available on both .NET and Java, with the most advanced inferencing algorithm on the market (Optimized Rete or Rete III), in addition to the unique compiled sequential mode optimized for sequential rule execution. COBOL code generation ensures that legacy CICS/mainframe environments can leverage business rules with maximum performance. In addition, Blaze Advisor allows for different, appropriate, rule evaluation modes for each rule set, providing both flexibility and performance.

Extensive integration capability

Blaze Advisor has a strong commitment to standards and open technologies across Java, .NET and COBOL. In the Java world, it supports J2SE and J2EE, along with WebSphere, WebLogic, Sun ONE, Oracle and JBoss application servers. It allows reading and writing of data from all leading SQL databases, XML schemas/documents, and external web services. It is easy to integrate with Business Process Management Systems and offers integrations with FileNet, Lombardi, Metastorm, DST, webMethods, Savvion, Fujitsu, Oracle BPEL and more. With Blaze Advisor, you will not have to change your environment to take advantage of business rules. In addition, Blaze Advisor prides itself on having a small memory "footprint."

Patented rule management application generation

The rule management applications generated from Blaze Advisor, based on its patented template technology, provide unique interfaces specifically designed for business user rule authoring and collaboration. Rule maintenance is done once and deployed anywhere through the shared repository. This enables both business and information technology (IT) professionals to effectively manage the rules in a central repository, regardless of deployment complexity or management environment. Blaze Advisor rule maintenance applications allow controlled rule editing and creation by non-technical users through standard web technologies. These template-driven applications expose some or all of the rules for controlled editing by non-technical users.

Predictive analytic models

Fair Isaac's unique experience in combining business rules with powerful predictive analytic models is shown in the analytic integration offered by Blaze Advisor. Not only does this allow the mining of business rules from data, it also allows for executable predictive analytic models to be brought directly to bear in decision services for true enterprise decision management. Fair Isaac's analytic tools allow for the conversion of insight into action, through embedding executable rules and models directly into the decision services used by applications. These models might be predictive scorecards, decision trees, neural nets or rules derived from genetic algorithms. This is where the future lies: bringing true business intelligence to operational decision-making.

Blaze Advisor Customers

Blaze Advisor is in use at hundreds of companies and government agencies around the world, from banking and insurance to telecommunications and manufacturing; from underwriting and origination to fraud detection, taxes and network configuration. Organizations like Auto Club Group, California Department of Motor Vehicles, Walgreens Health Services, British Telecom, egg, Unitrin Kemper, First Data, The Hartford, Sun Microsystems, and Dell Financial Services all deliver 24x7, mission-critical production decision services through Blaze Advisor-based systems.

- Auto Club Group is using Blaze Advisor for precise and consistent property and casualty policy quotes and uniform underwriting decisions across seven states.

- At the California Department of Motor Vehicles, Blaze Advisor drives modernization of legacy systems to deliver $4 billion dollars in vehicle registration fee calculations that are accurate and consistent statewide.

- Unitrin Kemper uses Blaze Advisor for real-time, risk-based underwriting of new business, a lowered combined ratio, reduced underwriting losses, and improved targeting of new business.

- First Data Corporation uses Blaze Advisor™ business rules management system for "Merchant Scoring"—analyzing merchant and agent data for more than 4,000,000 merchants who process daily transactions for their customers.

- Sun Microsystems uses Blaze Advisor to minimize customers' information technology risks, by empowering over 9,000 people around the world to identify and mediate potential IT issues (system configurations, firmware and software patches) before they can affect system downtime.

- egg's award-winning Blaze Advisor system provides coordinated credit risk decisions, reducing the amount of manual interventions and reducing the time for rule change from 35 days to 2 days.

- British Telecom uses Blaze Advisor for its Transform Operations Support System. Blaze Advisor remotely configure the organization's network devices, based on customer orders and configuration requests.

- Air Products uses Blaze Advisor to ensure accuracy of material master creation for its SAP implementation – the largest in the world.

- Walgreens Health Services uses Blaze Advisor rules to alert a pharmacist to potential adverse drug interactions. Drug interaction rules may be based on patient age, other drugs being taken, length of dosage and time between dosages, and so forth.

- The Hartford uses Blaze Advisor to handle the risk assessment of the Automobile, Homeowner and Umbrella lines of business from quoting to issuing to endorsing the final policy.

- Dell Financial Services (DFS) has implemented an enterprise policy hub using Blaze Advisor for continuous pricing—risk-based pricing of credit lines with suggested alternatives in real time.

Definition of an Enterprise Policy Hub

According to IDC, "The policy hub is that point in a business process at which decisions are made and from which the results of the decision are communicated to the people and business transactional/operational systems that are affected."[32]

An enterprise policy hub, sometimes called a universal decision engine, is a platform that delivers the results of operational decisions to the front-line transactional/operational systems and business processes. An enterprise policy hub centralizes an organization's operating policies, procedures, regulations, models, and expertise, delivering them *operationally* to all systems throughout the extended enterprise. It is the place where any process or system goes to get operational decisions made.

The delivery of an enterprise policy hub becomes possible when an organization decides to manage business policies, regulatory compliance, and business expertise as valued, reusable, and changing corporate assets. The enterprise policy hub concept is inherently compatible with current services-oriented architectures (SOA).

An organization's business policies and procedures define who they are as a business. For example, an organization lending money for automobile purchases indirectly defines who it is by how its personnel interact with potential customers, how it rates credit risk, and, therefore, how it prices services. The organization may either have policies and procedures that best support only low-risk customers, they offer products and services that cater to high-risk clients, or both, but it's the business rules that effectively define the customer-base. For example, business rules that offer competitive interest rates only to customers with very

---

32. Morris, Henry, and Dan Vesset. "Policy Hubs: Progress Toward Decision-Centric BI," IDC.

high FICO® scores are implicitly defining a market segment. Customers with lower FICO® scores who are offered non-competitive rates are effectively shunned.

An enterprise policy hub can be logical or physical. An organization might have a common set of APIs and calls that handle all decisions. Or, it might use a standard SOA environment to manage a set of decision services by building all of them in a BRMS like Blaze Advisor. A typical heterogeneous IT environment is likely to be a mixture—a single BRMS and rule repository with deployments as services and components in traditional architectures (Java, .NET or COBOL).

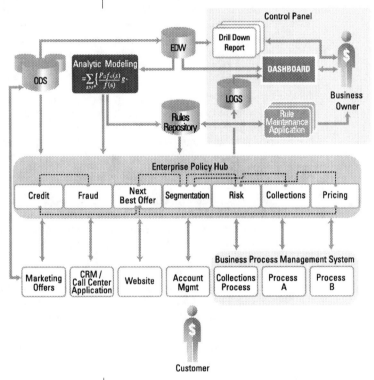

Figure 34: Overview of an Enterprise Policy Hub

An enterprise policy hub, as illustrated in Figure 34, delivers precise, consistent, and agile decisioning to all applications and processes throughout an enterprise. An enterprise policy hub has five key elements. First, there is a logical or physical service or set of services that deliver decisions to operational systems. In a pure SOA environment this might be an actual decision service or services, but in a more heterogeneous environment it consists of services, Java or .NET components and even COBOL programs deployed without a services wrapper. Regardless of the implementation approach, the enterprise policy hub has the responsibility for responding to requests for decisions on behalf of the enterprise in a consistent manner, regardless of request origin.

Second, the enterprise policy hub must be able to answer requests for the core operational decisions required by other systems. These decisions, such as assessing credit or calculating the next best offer, will often be used by multiple systems, will interact with each other, and may share rules. The enterprise policy hub must make it easy to share common rules effectively, and must ensure consistency of response across different systems and different implementation environments.

Third, operational data must be directly available to the enterprise policy hub. It can rely on information passed with the request, but should also be able to reach out to operational stores and even external sources for additional data required to make the appropriate decision.

Fourth, the enterprise policy hub is driven from an enterprise rules repository (physical or logical). The rules in this repository are managed in collaborative fashion by the business and IT. Business owners will use a performance management dashboard to monitor the business—both the behavior of the enterprise policy hub itself in the form of decision logs, and corresponding changes to rules. This might involve adding, changing, or removing rules, and will take advantage of the full range of rule authoring, rule versioning, release management, and other features offered by the repository.

Fifth, the enterprise policy hub is also the deployment infrastructure for predictive analytic models. As analysts and business users mine data for business rules (e.g. segmentation rules derived from customer data), or use data to build predictive models (e.g. a predictive scorecard for retention risk), these will be deployed into the decisioning framework that implements the enterprise policy hub. Not only does this allow the analyses to be deployed to operational systems, it allows new rules that take advantage of these insights, ensures consistency of usage of models, and maximizes return on investment (ROI) by guaranteeing that the analytically-enhanced decision is re-used across the enterprise.

Lastly there must be a control panel for the enterprise policy hub, a place where the business can control its behavior. This will typically be integrated with corporate performance management dashboards and other reports. By delivering rule maintenance alongside these measurement tools, the business can go from tracking behavior to controlling and managing behavior. This is when the new kind of business future begins—when true business intelligence guides operational decisions in the hands of business leaders.

The Benefits of an Enterprise Policy Hub

The benefits of an enterprise policy hub are many:

- Separation of core business logic
- Consistency and agility
- Precision
- Reusable business logic
- Competitiveness and profitability

Separation of core business logic

An enterprise policy hub extends the benefit of separating business rules (core business knowledge) from applications throughout the enterprise. Although the tactical Business Rules Approach separates high-value business rules from applications, only an enterprise-wide approach will do so with smaller groups of rules in minor applications. Without the enterprise approach, it is unlikely that a BRMS will be part of the tactical solution if only a few rules are re-usable or required by an application. However, if an enterprise policy hub is in place, many projects find it worthwhile to externalize, manage, and leverage business rules, bringing the proven benefits of business rules to a higher percentage of the application portfolio.

Consistency and agility

An enterprise policy hub is designed to provide consistency *with* agility. By centralizing operational decision-making, it helps guarantee consistent decision-making enterprise-wide. By using the Business Rules Approach and a BRMS to manage these decisions, it ensures that this consistency does not come at the expense of business agility. Modifications to the business policies are made once and, once deployed, are available via the rule service to the entire enterprise. With a combination of pressures to both demonstrate compliance with an ever-increasing array of regulations and more aggressive and faster-moving competitors, business agility must be maintained, but in an auditable, controlled, and compliant way.

Precision

One of the challenges facing many companies today is how to apply business intelligence to operational systems. An enterprise policy hub provides a platform for injecting precision into operational decision-making. With a single place to go for a particular decision, and a clear structure of how that decision is made, it is much easier to identify potential uses of information to improve decisions. Mining data for new rules or thresholds and embedding predictive analytic models to enhance the data available for decisioning enables new, more sophisticated rules behind automated decisions in the enterprise policy hub.

Reusable business logic

An enterprise policy hub truly enables an organization to treat logic as a reusable enterprise resource, to be managed and exploited. When the organization adds customer interaction channels, those channels can reuse all or part of the decision-making infrastructure to ensure rapid set-up and consistency. By automating decisions the organization can empower customers, partners, and employees to self-serve, and so reduce costs and improve service. By focusing human resources on the 5% of a decision that cannot, and perhaps should not, be completely automated, the organization can better leverage the experience and intelligence of its staff. By controlling the key decision-making points in operational processes, an organization is best positioned to in-source or outsource as needed.

Competitiveness and profitability

Decision making is a critical process to organizations seeking to improve competitiveness and profitability. Since many types of decisions are recurring or repeatable (such as pricing, extending credit, or allocating resources), decision-making processes exist that are amenable to automation. One benefit to decision process automation is that it enables greater consistency in the way decisions are made. This is important, not only for competitive reasons, but also increasingly for compliance reasons. As IDC said, "Companies must demonstrate that decisions were not arbitrary but followed established procedures. Hence, they require an auditable record of decisions and a defined decision process." [33]

Best Practices in Implementing an Enterprise Policy Hub

While there are huge benefits to be gained by implementing an enterprise policy hub, most organizations cannot and do not take on large projects that take too long to show a return. Implementing an enterprise policy hub must therefore generate an ROI at each stage. The following staged approach allows for incremental ROI and for a gradual increase in complexity where the experience in each stage helps reduce risk in the next.

Stage 1: Identify the potential decision services within your enterprise and begin establishing knowledge management processes to capture and engineer business rules. Identify enough of these processes to identify high-value decision services, the experts who understand them, and the legacy systems that must be considered. It is essential to find the right first project and to start as you mean to go on—considering rules as a corporate asset.

Having found the right first project, create value with an initial decision service. This requires two parallel activities. One activity is to implement rules locally in

---

33. *Ibid.*

a high value service/system, to generate an immediate ROI for a system or service that is suitable for business rules automation. These typically:

a. Have lots of rules—hundreds, thousands or more.

b. Have rules that change often—perhaps weekly or daily.

c. Have rules that are very complex, making coding them difficult.

d. Have rules that require domain expertise to be understood, making it valuable to have the business users author them to reduce errors.

The second activity, done simultaneously with the first, is to design an enterprise rules repository. Even if the organization starts with a single project to show ROI and develop experience, it must invest in designing the repository for enterprise use. This is akin to designing services, not just for their first use, but for subsequent ones and their likely relationship to future services.

Notes on repository design

There are some general organizational guidelines for repository architecture. In general, there are four main components: a business library, technical library, rule services library and testing library.

- Business Library: Contains the business rules maintained by the business users using the rule maintenance application, and is organized in a way that follows a natural navigation scheme for the business users.
- Technical Library: Contains the technical "infrastructure" entities created and maintained by technical users using the IDE. It typically includes entities such as the object definitions, overall rule flow, and the templates that will control what business users can edit. The Technical Library content is typically managed by the rules architect and rules developers. Typically, groups of related services will have common object models and templates.
- Rules Services Library: Contains everything deployed in the production application(s); describes the external interface to the rule service (the data required and returned) and also specifies which repository entities make up this rule/decision service, typically assembling all or part of the Technical Library and some Business Library folders.
- Testing Library: Contains the rules services to be unit tested, test data, a mechanism to load test data from a data warehouse, and a test rule flow that strings together one or more rules services for testing.

Stage 2: Find opportunities to reuse rules. A high-quality SOA enables reuse of services. In addition, some rules from first projects can often be reused in other systems. Sometimes a whole rule service can be reused (either as a service in the SOA-sense or by regenerating the rules into a new deployment for a different platform). However, often only some of the rules will be reusable. For instance, there might be another opportunity to use customer segmentation rules or dispute rating rules. It may well be that there is a need to replace old code or add additional functionality to old systems. This can often be justified by reducing ongoing costs (by reducing or eliminating maintenance) or adding value (better targeted cross-sell, resulting in additional revenue).

The first opportunities to reuse rules will likely require re-factoring unless there is a very stable and well-defined object model. Those organizations well on the way to a model-driven approach should have object models that are sufficiently well-defined to make this straightforward. Others may have to allow for re-factoring time.

Stage 3: Identify business/elemental services under development or in planning that are "decision-centric." Automate them using the rules platform. This is an ongoing activity for those organizations adopting SOA. Business services are often decision-centric and meet the criteria outlined above—many rules, complex rules, changeable rules or business-centric rules. The rules platform should be used for these. These services need governance and management above and beyond that offered for other services, as the business users will be collaborating in changing the services and the services will likely change more often.

Stage 4: Encourage the business groups responsible for the rules to start to feel accountability for the decisions and the decision engine, not just the rules or logic. This is a more advanced step. Essentially, you want those groups who define how decisions are made (such as credit analysts with credit policies or underwriters with underwriting guidelines) to be responsible to the enterprise, not only for the policies, but for the decision engine itself.

Stage 5: Leverage predictive analyses to improve rules. There is a huge potential for analyses in this context. Not only can analytic techniques be used to find better rules, e.g. by mining data, they can also be used to enhance the information available to rules. Thus, mining a set of data about customer behavior

Chapter 13: Implementing an Enterprise Policy Hub

can produce statistically significant segmentation rules, aimed at a retention score showing how "at risk" a customer is. The next step is to define additional rules to handle effectively these risk customers.

Integrating an Enterprise Policy Hub with BPM, SOA, and BI

One of the great advantages to an enterprise policy hub is that it adds value to and works with core technology adoption trends, not against them.

An enterprise policy hub ensures simplicity of process definitions in a BPMS by keeping decision complexity out. Decisions are handled by a decisioning backbone leaving the process environment to handle process definition and execution. This also allows for the same decision to be made consistently across the enterprise and/or multiple BPMS implementations, and between BPMS and other systems.

This approach also provides a platform for operationalizing business intelligence (BI). One of the challenges with most BI approaches is that applying the insight gained from data to the day-to- day (or second-to-second) operational decisions is hard. Most people do not find it easy to use OLAP cubes or advanced visualization and analysis tools. Automating decisions across the enterprise creates a platform for using insight to improve decisions over time. Because the decision logic is encapsulated and managed, it can be changed based on new analysis, or enhanced with new analytic models without impacting the systems that rely on it.

If an organization is adopting an SOA approach, a subset of all business services will be delivered through your enterprise policy hub. These services can then be managed as atomic services (something your SOA environment does), but also in terms of the *regulations, policies,* and *procedures* that define your business. These services are most often the ones that must change, and the use of a business rules management system to automate them makes this change easier to manage. The use of an enterprise policy hub can also make it easier to guarantee consistency and compliance across channels, across business units, and across services.

An enterprise policy hub also enhances your performance management backbone by giving you points of pressure at which you can apply the insight gained from your performance management systems. There is, of course, no point in monitoring or measuring something you cannot readily change. An enterprise policy hub underpins the corporate performance management approach to make sure you can change what is not working.

Summary

While an organization can deploy a BRMS as a very significant programmer productivity tool and achieve great benefits, the greatest ROI becomes possible when automating and improving operational decisions across the enterprise. Blaze Advisor is a great solution, either way.

Finally, here are some words from Blaze Advisor customers.

"The most important thing that we would stress to other organizations is how important it is to have a strategic vision with an eye on the future."
Michael Koscielny, Director, Regional Underwriting Operations at ACG

"We were able to isolate our highest ROI component and renovate it with the best value."
Jerrianne Seitz, Data Processing and DMV Project Manager

"We have business people in the Underwriting Department managing our rules and managing the promotion of our rules into code."
Patrick Madigan, VP of Underwriting, Kemper Auto and Home

"To our knowledge, no other merchant processing system of this scale exists today that empowers such precision, consistency, agility and analytic rigor for decision management strategy implementation and execution."
Giancarlo Marchesi, senior vice president of Global Decision Management at First Data

"We got a full ROI on Blaze Advisor in six months, and we estimate it has generated £5 million in savings per year."
Phil Jobson, egg

More information on Blaze Advisor can be found at:
www.fairisaac.com/rulesbook
or by emailing:
edm@fairisaac.com

James Taylor authors blogs at www.edmblog.com and www.ebizq.net/blogs/decision management. Details on James' writing and speaking are available at www.aboutjt.com.

References

Morris, Henry, and Dan Vesset. "Policy Hubs: Progress Toward Decision-Centric BI," IDC.

14 Putting the Business Back in Business Rules

(A Source Rule Repository for RMM Level 2)

Barbara von Halle

The Significance of RMM Level 2

Most organizations included in the RMM Survey discussed in Chapter 2 listed agility as their top motivator for the Business Rules Approach. This is not surprising, if we remember what Charles Darwin once said, "It is not the strongest of the species that survive, nor the most intelligent, but the one most responsive to change." Thus, RMM Level 2 is the most commonly sought organizational or project target, as organizational agility truly begins at RMM Level 2. RMM Level 2 is also the *jumping-off point* for achieving higher levels of the RMM, and the level at which *today's* common practices, standards, and technology come together.

As a quick reminder, a Level 2 organization seeks agility in its rules. Not only does the organization need to *know* some of the rules, but wants to be able to *change* them on demand. Perhaps it wants to respond more quickly to threats or to opportunities.

Specifically, organizations aiming for RMM Level 2 will usually deploy a business rule management system (BRMS), because doing so achieves technical agility.

With a BRMS (from vendors such as ILOG and Fair Isaac), an RMM Level 2 organization can develop new rules and make rule changes faster than Level 0 or Level 1, because the technology enables changes, one rule or set of rules at a time. And this is done with minimal programming. The development time for systems with a BRMS is shorter and, more importantly, the maintenance cycle for rule changes can be *significantly* shorter.

The Greatest Challenge for RMM Level 2

The RMM Survey also pointed out that most organizations want to harvest business rules from business people, and they want to manage those rules from a business perspective. Survey participants often stated that, despite good intentions, rules delivered in systems, even with a BRMS, can become lost to the business again. That is, the business rules are buried again, and there isn't a clear way to measure the impact of business rule changes on various aspects of the business and systems.

Therefore, another important aspect of a true RMM Level 2 organization is to conduct impact analysis of potential rule changes on the business itself (not just its systems). After all, it makes little sense for an organization to make many rule changes quickly, without knowing how those changes are expected to impact processes, systems, and stakeholders.

Meeting the Challenge of RMM Level 2

Achieving RMM Level 2, therefore, means assessing business rule changes and changing the right rules quickly. This requires sufficient business-rule metadata to tie the business- relevant pieces together. It also requires traceability from the business rules to business- relevant models. Otherwise, the ability to do impact analysis about proposed rule changes is limited. This traceability is made possible by new software functionality that provides links from rules to all relevant business items.

The KPI STEP™ Workbench, available today, provides the separation and traceability required for achieving RMM Level 2 for business and IT audiences, independent of target implementation technology. The KPI STEP™ Workbench is the subject of this chapter. It is available with the KPI STEP™ License, which also includes methods, templates, training, and software support.

The remainder of the chapter covers:

- Sample best practices and standards today

- Enterprise architecture, the Zachman Framework, and business rules

- Separating business rules in a process chart

- Separating business rules in a use case

- The rule-rich decision as a critical business lever

- Business versus technical analysis of business rules

- Tracing business rules to process charts in the KPI STEP™ Workbench

- Tracing business rules to use cases in the KPI STEP™ Workbench

- Tracing object models to business rules in the KPI STEP™ Workbench

- Putting it all together and delivering Rule Maturity Model level 2

- Beyond Rule Maturity Model level 2

- Essential lessons learned

Sample Best Practices and Standards Today

RMM Level 2, because it is so critical to the continued success of the Business Rules Approach, needs to be easily attainable. Therefore, business rules in an RMM Level 2 organization or project must integrate smoothly with standard deliverables that are familiar to organizations today.

Consider the six important areas for which there are standard or common deliverables in Table 7.

Table 7: Six Practice Areas and Commonly Managed Deliverables

Practice Area	Sample Standard or Common Deliverables
Enterprise architecture	Zachman Framework for enterprise architecture
Business modeling	Process chart (swimlane diagram)
Use case modeling	Use case model
	Use case description
Object Modeling	UML model
Data Modeling	Entity-relationship model

Table 7: Six Practice Areas and Commonly Managed Deliverables (continued)

Practice Area	Sample Standard or Common Deliverables
Business Rules	Separated business rules
	Business-relevant business rule metadata
	Business and technical analysis of business rules
	Traceability of business rules to models and metadata
	Authoring and storing of technical rules
	Rule flow diagrams of technical rules
	Analysis of technical rules

A goal for Rule Maturity Model Level 2 is to seamlessly incorporate business rules into these common modeling and architecture techniques, while delivering the benefits and functionality of managing those rules. Let's explore these areas, starting with enterprise architecture.

Enterprise Architecture, the Zachman Framework, and Business Rules

Chapter 4, The Business Architecture of Business Rules Based Enterprises, proposes a logical relationship of business rules (in the Zachman Framework Column 6) and some of the other columns of the framework.

For example, Chapter 4 proposes that strategy and objectives belong in Column 6 of the Zachman Framework (Motivation) and Row 2 (Planner's Perspective). Rule families or sets of rules, rules in natural language, and a corresponding glossary belong in Column 6, Row 3 (Owner's Perspective). And, finally, designed rule sets belong in Column 6 Row 4 (Designer's Perspective).

Chapter 4 also advocates that all business rule deliverables be linked in meaningful ways and traceable to deliverables in the other columns. Thus, the Zachman Framework becomes a foundation for designing the traceability needed for achieving Rule Maturity Model Level 2.

Rather than review these linkages in detail, it is important to understand how the linkages should occur, based on standard or common deliverables in the columns of the Zachman Framework. The starting point is the Function Column, representing function or process deliverables. Because most participants in the RMM Survey are using process modeling techniques and use cases, this chapter explores separating and tracing business rules to these deliverables.

Separating Business Rules in a Process Chart

Figure 35 depicts a process chart, sometimes called a swimlane diagram. A process chart consists of a starting event (e.g., a customer requests a loan) and an ending event (e.g., a customer loan is approved). In between those events are processes or tasks that are performed in a prescribed sequence and by specific parties. In Figure 35, there are two processes (i.e., process 1 and process 2) performed by the Applicant and one process (i.e., process 3) performed by the Loan Department.

Separating Business Rules in a Process Chart

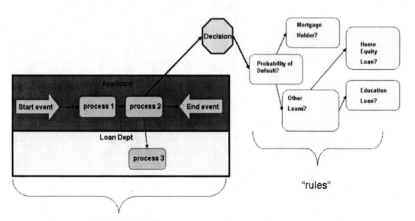

"rules"

"process chart"

Figure 35:   Business Rules and Process Charts

A process chart should say nothing about business rules, other than illustrating where rules are to guide the processes. A common, but bad, practice is to bury the business rules in the descriptions behind the process boxes. This is bad because the rules are buried too deep for traceability and for true impact analysis, delivering, at most, an RMM Level 0 process.

On the right in Figure 35, the rules are in the yellow boxes. Each yellow box represents a set of rules, so there are five sets of rules. For example, the box labeled "Probability of Default?" is the set of rules that determines whether an applicant is likely to default on a loan. The box labeled "Mortgage Holder?" is the set of rules that determines whether an applicant has an active mortgage.

There are arrows among these rule sets. The arrows represent dependencies among them. So, for example, the rule set that determines if the applicant has a home equity loan provides input to the rule set that determines if the applicant has other loans.

In Figure 35, the whole entire collection of these rule sets are organized together under the green box, called a Decision. Organizing whole sets of rules under one decision, in a rigorous manner, allows a process box to be connected to one decision with all of its underlying rules. The decision can also be connected to all relevant process boxes in all relevant process charts. In this way, all of the rules are then linked to these models in this manner, through the use of one decision anchor point. The decision separates the rules from the process chart, allowing changes to the rules in the decision to be independent of changes in the process chart and vice versa.

Separating Business Rules in a Use Case

Figure 36 illustrates the details behind a use case. The use case has a name, shown in the red bubble, which is "Pre-qualify Loan Request." The blue boxes depict the detailed steps behind this use case.

Like the previous process chart, a use case should say nothing about business rules, other than to indicate which steps in it are guided by rules. A bad practice would be to bury the rules in the use case description or within the documentation for each use case step. Again, this buries them too deep for traceability and for impact analysis, creating an RMM Level 0 use case.

Separating Business Rules in a Use Case

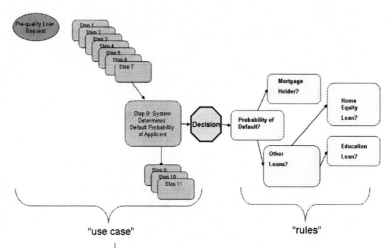

Figure 36:   Business Rules and Use Cases

On the right in Figure 36, in yellow, is the same collection of related rule sets from Figure 35. However, in Figure 36, these rule sets are anchored through the green Decision to Step 8 of the use case, which is "System Determines Default Probability of Applicant." So, the same rules behind the decision enables the decision to be linked to the use case step. This means that changes in the use case steps can be independent of changes in the rules themselves.

But there is one more benefit to appreciate. What if the same decision, as a collection of rule sets, is relevant to a step in a use case *and* to a process box in a process chart? The decision, which groups all relevant rules together, can serve as the common anchor point for those rules in any kind of process model deliverables, from process charts to use cases to activity diagrams.

An added benefit is that this common linkage also encourages consistent application of decisions across many different kinds of model-oriented deliverables, thereby also supporting the consistency goal for Rule Maturity Model Level 3.

The Rule-Rich Decision As a Critical Business Lever

It turns out that decisions are really running the company, whether those decisions are strategic ones or tactical ones, and whether or not they are carried out appropriately, automated or not.

Decisions are therefore important to the business and can be managed as such. They become visible to customers, because decisions determine how you interface with each customer. If an important decision is done incorrectly or inconsistently, it can cost money or cause regulatory violations. Decisions, made tangible and manageable, bring the business people closer to the way decisions drive business. Decisions, as collections of rules, are where the business can start to fine-tune itself by changing one rule at a time and determining the impact of that change.

Finally, decisions fit seamlessly into any modeling technique, done properly, not just process models.

The decision, therefore, emerges as the standard link, starting with RMM Level 1. The decision in the KPI STEP ™ Workbench is how business rules are separated from all other kinds of models.

Business vs. Technical Analysis of Business Rules

To better understand the importance of the decision as the business rule anchor point, consider the distinction between what we call *business* analysis of business rules and *technical* analysis of business rules.

Business analysis of business rules means being able to answer questions such as the following:

- Where is a particular decision operating in the business today? Which processes, systems, use cases, etc. are part of that decision?

- What objectives are to be achieved by a particular decision? How close are you to attaining those objectives?

- What metrics are associated with a particular business process? Which business rules are put into place within that business process in order to achieve or exceed those metrics?

- If you change a particular business objective, which rules need to change, and who will be impacted by that change?

Sophisticated traceability from business rules to business-related metadata is needed to answer these questions.

On the other hand, technical analysis of business rules means being able to answer questions such as the following:

- Which rule sets are incomplete, have inconsistencies, or have overlaps?

- Which business rules require which attributes in an object model?

- Who is empowered to change a rule in a production system?

Traceability from business rules to technically-related metadata and to semantics is needed to answer these questions.

Tracing Business Rules to Process Charts in the KPI STEP™ Workbench

Figure 37 contains a set of screens from the KPI STEP™ Workbench. Screen 1 contains a browser listing of items in this repository. Scrolling through the browser, a decision is selected because the decision is the subject of potential change. In this case, it is the decision called "Determine the Default Probability of Applicant."

In Screen 2, this decision is referenced by three different factors: use case steps, business rules, and elementary business processes. So, changing anything about the decision, such as its objectives or rules, will impact all of these factors.

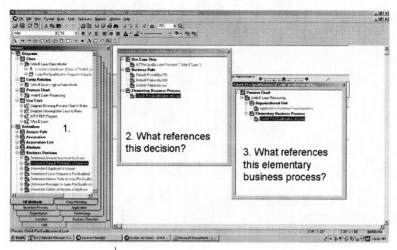

Figure 37: Tracing Business Rules to Process Charts

In Screen 3, the selected elementary business process from Screen 2 is shown to be part of the process chart called "Web-E Loan Processing" and is referenced in the swimlane assigned to the "Applicant or Customer Representative."

If the decision had been referenced in more than one process chart, the process charts would be disclosed, providing an understanding of the full impact of changing anything about that decision on process charts.

Tracing Business Rules to Use Cases in the KPI STEP™ Workbench

Screen 1, in Figure 38, contains the same browser listing of items in the repository as in Figure 37, with the same decision highlighted. Again, in Screen 2, this decision is referenced by three different factors: use case steps, business rules, and elementary business processes.

Tracing Business Rules to Use Cases

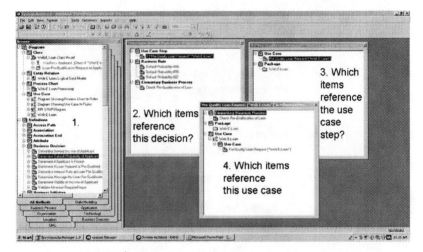

Figure 38: Tracing Business Rules to Use Cases

However, this time, in Screen 3, you see that the referenced use case step in Screen 2 is part of the use case called "Pre-Qualify Loan Request" and the package "Web-E Loan."

Again, if the decision had been referenced in more than one use case, these would be disclosed, providing a full impact on use cases of changing anything about that decision.

Screen 4 discloses that the use case is referenced by the elementary business process called "Check Pre-Qualification of Loan." This traceability has become intriguing.

It seems that someone has attached this use case to this particular process box in a process chart. It all begins to make sense.

During scoping, an analyst may attach decisions to a box in a process chart to set the stage for rule harvesting. Later, as part of detailed requirements or design, the decisions can be assigned to steps in a use case, as appropriate. In fact, the rules behind the decision can be added at any time, actually.

Tracing Object Models to Business Rules in the KPI STEP™ Workbench

Figure 39 illustrates the traceability from an attribute in an object model to business rules.

Tracing Object Models to Business Rules

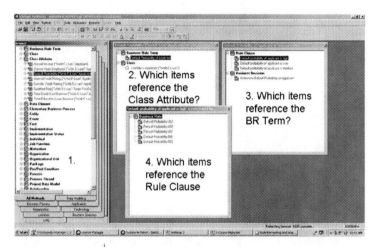

Figure 39: Tracing Object Models to Business Rules

In screen 1, a class attribute, "default probability," is selected. Screen 2 discloses that this class attribute is connected to a business rule term, "Default Probability of Applicant," and to a class, representing an entity called "Applicant."

Screen 3 further discloses that this business rule term is referenced by three rule clauses (which can be conditions or conclusions in rules) and by one decision. These rule clauses are "Default probability of applicant is High," "Default probability of applicant is Medium," and "Default probability of applicant is Low."

So the business term, represented by the selected class attribute, is used in three rule clauses and is the result of one decision.

Screen 4 illustrates the items that reference one of the rule clauses, and, specifically, five business rules that contain this clause, either as a condition or a conclusion.

Therefore, a change in that class attribute, such as its data type or set of allowable values, may impact five business rules and one decision. There is even more to know with sophisticated traceability.

Once the traceability leads to a decision that will be impacted by a change, the decision is the anchor point to all process models and use cases. So the corresponding process charts, use cases, and any other models impacted by a change in this decision or its rules can be disclosed. Also, not shown here, is traceability to stakeholders, so you can notify people of pending changes.

And this is just the beginning. Any models can be connected in this way, to the same rules, the same decisions and the same terms. This is how the power of sophisticated business rule traceability and impact analysis becomes possible, and when business rule changes can be assessed for impact analysis before they are deployed in a manual process or BRMS, for example.

Pulling It All Together and Delivering Rule Maturity Model Level 2

The table in Figure 40 lists the common and standard deliverables from Table 7. The third column indicates that the first four of these deliverables are very well supported with today's modeling and requirements tool suites. But, support for the business rule pieces is either lacking or minimal with such products.

The fourth column indicates the business rule support provided by most BRMS products. However, traceability from models to the business-relevant business rule metadata is usually lacking in these products.

So, there is an important gap: a barrier to achieving full RMM Level 2 benefits.

The fifth column of Figure 40 fills the gap. It represents the software functionality available with KPI's STEP™ Workbench. The combination of the KPI STEP™ Workbench and BRMS(s) covers all bases needed for RMM Level 2. There is now an unbroken business rule continuum.

Practice Area	Sample Standards or Best Practice	Modeling and Requirements Tool Suites	BRE/ BRMS	KPI STEP™ WB
Business Modeling	Process Chart (swimlane)	X	X-some	X
Use Case Modeling	Use Case Model and Description	X		X
Object Modeling	UML	X	X-some	X
Data Modeling	Entity Relationship Model	X		X
Business Rules	Separate BRs	X-some	X	X
	Provide robust BR metadata			X
	Trace BRs to models and metadata			X
	Business analysis of BR			X
	Enable authoring and storing of technical rules		X	
	Generate rule flow diagrams of technical rules		X	
	Perform analysis of technical rules		X	

Figure 40: Essential Functionality for RMM Level 2

Beyond Rule Maturity Model Level 2

Achieving higher levels of the RMM requires more sophisticated software. Today, organizations aiming for or achieving Rule Maturity Model Level 3 and higher usually develop their own software. But the vision for such software is in the Rule Maturity Model and evolution of commercial software will follow the demand.

Summary and Lessons Learned from RMM Level 2 Software

For most readers of this book, RMM Level 2 is an appropriate goal that delivers many promises of the Business Rules Approach. RMM Level 2 aims for knowledge and agility of rules. For the knowledge part, the source rule repository needs to store rules, at least in business-friendly form, with terms and rule clauses and grouped by decisions.

But for the agility part, the source rule repository must enable fast rule changes. Fast rule changes are possible to the technical rules in the BRMS, but the impact of those changes on the business requires more metadata and traceability. Specifically, RMM Level 2 demands traceability from business motivations to rules, from rules to process models and use cases and systems, from data elements and class attributes to rules, and from rules to stakeholders. The RMM Level 2 source rule repository provides comprehensive traceability at business fingertips.

Essential Lessons Learned

- Comprehensive traceability ensures that the impact of rule changes is known ahead of time.

- Comprehensive traceability ensures that all relevant stakeholders are notified, can discuss, and are prepared for rule changes before they happen.

- Traceability needs to be provided to every possible deliverable an organization creates.

- Re-use of terms, rule clauses, and rules in a source rule repository saves time and minimizes errors.

- The connection of business relevant items (e.g. motivations, decisions, stakeholders, rules, and terms) to technical relevant items (e.g. data models, object models) allows business and technical people to use the same source rule repository.

- The source rule repository needs to be fully customizable to the organization's or project's methods and standards.

And looking a bit further an RMM Level 3 source rule repository will provide:

- Sophisticated security and authorization capabilities.

- Workflow management for the entire business rule life cycle (i.e., roles, authorizations, tutorials, and queue management).

- Integration with testing and simulating capabilities.

- Separation but integration with BRMSs, so as to remain agnostic to target platform and be useable across many platforms and for non-automated rules.

- Integration with full repositories, so as to share models and deliverables across multiple tools, even within one organization.

- Management dashboards to assess the status of current and future rule sets.

When these are so, the promises of RMM Level 3 are just around the corner. Business leaders will truly navigate the business, powered safely by its changing business rules.

Part IV
Wrap Up

It seems most fitting that we end this book with a look at innovations that are changing the world as we once knew it and also how the Business Rules Approach will play such a role. We close also with highlights from our valued book supporters.

"The alternative is to drift into the storm and to be lost at sea."

Chapter 15, Larry Goldberg

The Time is Now: The Economic Imperative for the Business Rules Approach

Larry Goldberg

One of the great innovations of modern times is the joint stock company. So much of the wealth of the world has been created because of this simple but ingenious solution to the issue of individual investment risk.

As a consequence of the extraordinary success of this evolution of human organization, particularly in the great free-market economies of the West, corporations have evolved into immense organizations of great complexity. Economies of the First World have thrived, generating wealth unrivaled in the history of the world.

Not just in the First World. The real story today is that global economic growth is reaching historic highs, and the engines of growth lie beyond the borders of the First World. Now that nations in the developing world are able to bypass historic and sometime circuitous evolution toward free markets, and are rapidly adopting the tools of the modern economy, new global economic powers are rapidly emerging. China, India, Russia, and other emerging nations are altering the balance of economic power. Corporate organizations, unknown heretofore, are suddenly household words: Lenovo, Tata, Rosneft.

What has this to do with a book about The Business Rules Revolution? Well, everything.

New forces are afoot in the world. As large, and as complex, as our organizations have become, they are going to have to react to the disruptive changes brought about by the emergence of the global economy. Outsourcing is only a tiny part of the story. a harbinger of the storm to come. Serious new competition in almost every field of endeavor will become the norm. Change in its revolutionary sense will become the imperative of survival and prosperity in this brave new world. This will impact not only for-profit based organizations. Government and Non-Government Organizations (NGOs) will be equally challenged to change with the arrival of the storm. And change is not easy when we are in large organizations that have evolved over decades.

During the most recent period of technologic disruption, the advent of the Internet, we saw great successes amongst those organizations that were able to rapidly adjust to change, and the eclipsing of those that were incapable of agility by tiny upstart rivals. As great an upheaval as technology disruption may be, it pales against the forces of economic disruption.

So we believe that agility is the single most important quality for a competitive organization. Not technological agility, a necessary but insufficient condition, but business agility.

How does the business achieve agility when most operating platforms today are based on large legacy information systems, many of them built decades ago, where the processes and logic of the system are deeply buried beneath many layers of history, like the remnants of ancient cities that lie beneath the sands of time?

We don't propose glib answers to this crucial question. But in this book the discerning reader should have grasped an outline of a path towards greater agility. The great promise of the Business Rules Approach is corporate agility, but it is clear that there are many steps along the path that must be taken, one by one, to reach the goal.

At first there is the business decision to take this approach: a crucial step and one that needs to engage many facets of the organization.

Then there is the architectural preparation, planning at every level of the organization for the implementation of change. This may involve a considerable amount of archeology to discern what the organization has become, and what lies under the sands. And it requires a vision for the future of each and every aspect of the business, and a structural plan of how this can be achieved.

Then comes the technology planning. The future of the technology is exciting in and of itself. Your editors invited two leading technology vendors to propose their vision of the future (which can be found later in this chapter), and these visions, while somewhat divergent, point to technology that can truly enable organizational agility. These solutions and others from the wider community of vendors will continue to evolve: the ability of the business to deploy them to do its bidding will in the end depend upon the maturity of its approach, not only in technology, but in business governance and control. Therefore, we also invited a leading Business Rules services vendor to summarize how they support Business Rules technology and governance projects.

Execution at both the business level and the technology level is crucial. The Business Rules Approach, in order to achieve business agility, needs to acquire a relatively advanced level of maturity. Some tension may have been detected in the degree of business control implied in several of the chapters in this book. This is a natural reflection of divergence in the level of maturity of the approach. It is almost essential in many cases for IT professionals to lead the way in this new endeavor. Over time, as the capabilities of the enabling technology mature, so does the business professional fully grasp the reins of control over the business rules. This may have to be the nature of the journey.

Ultimately, however, management is going to have to grasp control of the business rules to both envision a future state and to make the rapid course corrections that will be necessary to achieve that future state. The alternative is to drift into the storm, and to be lost at sea.

Fair Isaac

Fair Isaac Corporation (NYSE:FIC) helps businesses improve their decision-making.. The company's solutions and technologies for enterprise decision management give businesses the power to automate more processes and apply more intelligence to every customer interaction. By increasing the precision, consistency and agility of their decisions, Fair Isaac clients throughout the world increase sales, build customer value, cut fraud losses, manage credit risk, reduce operational costs, meet changing compliance demands and enter new markets more profitably.

Founded in 1956, Fair Isaac powers hundreds of billions of decisions a year in financial services, insurance, telecommunications, retail, consumer-branded goods, healthcare and the public sector. Fair Isaac also helps millions of U.S. individuals manage their credit health through the www.myfico.com website.

Your business decisions are your next critical source of value. But making the best decisions is well beyond the capacity of most business systems today, when decisions must be made faster, across more channels and product lines, leveraging more data, under greater regulatory demands and competitive pressures, and with more complicated constraints and trade-offs. The best way to meet these demands is through a common decision management infrastructure that serves multiple processes and systems.

This is why businesses are embracing the discipline known as enterprise decision management (EDM)—a systematic approach to automating and improving decisions. Through business rules management technology, advanced predictive analytics and more effective use of data, EDM increases the precision, consistency and agility of operational business decisions.

Fair Isaac provides enterprise decision management solutions that integrate predictive analysis with business rules management to automate and improve decisions in customer management and other areas. Among these solutions are the systems used to manage two-thirds of the world's credit cards, and protect them from fraudulent activity. Fair Isaac also provides tools and services that help businesses develop and deploy their own systems for enterprise decision management.

Fair Isaac (continued)

Fair Isaac is recognized as the leading company in enterprise decision management, with the most comprehensive portfolio of industry solutions and advanced technologies. Our approach to EDM gives your existing information management systems—data warehousing, business intelligence, existing applications—the intelligence you need to operate on your "efficient frontier," where risks, costs and losses are minimized, while efficiency, customer service, ROI and profit are maximized.

Our market-leading EDM Applications span the customer lifecycle—including marketing, originations, customer management, collections and recovery, and fraud management—and are available for specific processes in financial services, insurance, telecommunications, retail and healthcare. We also offer the most sophisticated EDM technology, including the Blaze Advisor™ business rules management system, model development tools, custom analysis and other services. You can design your EDM architecture using the same technology we use to build and deploy our EDM Applications, or rely on our expertise to create a custom application for your needs.

Because Fair Isaac applications are based on a common EDM technology platform, businesses can integrate, extend and expand their EDM architecture, which reduces development, maintenance, and training costs while enabling true lifecycle customer management.

The Blaze Advisor™ business rules management system is a comprehensive, advanced rules management solution that covers the entire process for developing, deploying and maintaining rules-based business applications. This leading-edge technology radically improves the way enterprises manage business applications and processes by enabling them to develop complex applications faster, respond quickly to changing business factors, and reduce the total cost of day-to-day operations.

Visit Fair Isaac online at www.fairisaac.com

Learn more about Blaze Advisor at www.fairisaac.com/rules

Read the EDM blog at http://edmblog.fairisaac.com

Request more information by E-mailing edm@fairisaac.com or calling 1-888-FICO-EDM (+1 408 535 1500).

Next Steps or How to Get Started Now—ILOG Excerpt

Given that ILOG's mission as a company is to deliver software and services that empower its customers to make better decisions and manage change faster, it is understandable why ILOG has worked so hard to make JRules™ the market-leading business rule management system (BRMS). JRules makes business rule management practical by providing innovative tools to author, deploy, and manage business rules across the whole spectrum of policy-intensive applications present in the modern enterprise. In so doing, JRules has become an essential part of the IT infrastructures of hundreds of businesses worldwide. Besides Equifax, customers of the award-winning JRules include eBay, Grupo Santander, Harrah's Entertainment, Visa, Vodafone, Zurich, and many other leading *Global 2000* companies and governments.

ILOG has consistently built on its history of product innovation to make JRules the industry's leading business rule software. Gartner Dataquest ranked ILOG the market share leader of the worldwide business rule engine software market for 2004, and positioned ILOG in the leader quadrant of Gartner's 2005 Magic Quadrant for Business Rule Engines. The company has also been twice-named the BRMS market leader by IT research firm IDC.

With JRules 6, ILOG has produced the first BRMS to provide enterprise business rule management without compromise:

- Full empowerment for business teams
- Full productivity for tech teams
- Synchronized full life-cycle business rule management
- Unequalled performance

Because JRules 6 requires no compromises, it is able to deliver the fastest time-to-business value and lowest total cost of ownership of any BRMS.

More information on ILOG JRules including datasheets, case studies and white papers can be obtained from ILOG's BRMS web pages at brms.ilog.com. To speak to an ILOG representative directly by phone call 1-800-FOR-ILOG

InScope Solutions

InScope Solutions is a trusted advisor to clients in the federal, commercial, and non-profit sectors. We pursue business, engineering, and technology solutions that transform, inspire, and advance the success of our clients.

This pursuit has led us into business rule solutions, naturally. By assembling world-class expertise and best practices, InScope Solutions is well-positioned to assist your enterprise in deploying sound and successful business rule management systems.

We believe that it is important to view the adoption of the Business Rules Approach from an enterprise perspective. Initiating the adoption process with a consolidated, global view is crucial to fully realizing the vision of business rules as a true corporate asset.

This global outlook encompasses all phases of development as the business rule capabilities of an enterprise mature:

- Enhanced business value, by understanding what the rules are, how they should be captured, where they should be documented, and how they ultimately fit into system requirements.
- A sound technical state, emphasizing quality and consistency through the implementation cycle.
- Facilitated business control, by creating an environment that has the right people, processes, and systems in place to accommodate rapid change.

We don't do this alone. InScope Solutions has partnered with leading BRMS vendors and business rule practitioners to craft a complete methodology, bound together by our industry-tested approach for business rule governance.

InScope Solutions has a prestigious list of clients, including both defense and civilian government agencies, non-profit organizations, and commercial enterprises, including several *Fortune 500* members. InScope has been identified by CMP Media's CRN as the eleventh fastest growing solution provider in the nation and #1 in the Washington, DC-metropolitan region for the period 2003 to 2005.

More information on InScope Solutions may be found on our website at http://www.inscopesolutions.com/.

Information specific to our Business Rule Practice, including white papers, can be obtained at http://rules.inscopesolutions.com/.

To speak to an InScope Solutions representative directly, please call 1-703-391-1990.

About Knowledge Partners, Inc.

Knowledge Partners, Inc. (KPI) has—since its founding by Barbara von Halle in 1997—been one of the industry's premier thought-leadership company in the business rules sphere.

In 2001 KPI completed a seminal book on the practice of business rules (Barbara von Halle, *Business Rules Applied*, New York: John Wiley & Sons, Inc., 2002) that laid out a foundation for a practical approach to business rules projects. While focused on providing methodologies, the book reflected KPI's commitment to achieving results rather than creating theoretical constructs. As a result of this down-to-earth, get-it-done approach, the book is a standard text in the field of business rules, and became a finalist for the 2002 CMP Media's Software Development Magazine Jolt award. Candidates for this award, which is reserved for "products, books, and websites that have jolted the industry by helping to create faster, easier, and more efficient software," are nominated by end-customers and finalists chosen by judges.

Other important milestones in KPI's long association with the Business Rules Approach include:

IBM® Rational Unified Process or RUP® Plug-in

KPI, in partnership with Fair Isaac Corporation, developed a business rules plug-in for RUP, still today the only defined business rules methodology for RUP available on the market.

Business Rules Mining Methodology

Working with clients and technology suppliers, KPI developed a comprehensive methodology to mine business rules from a disparate range of legacy systems. This methodology was incorporated into the KPI STEP™ License Program.

KPI Rule Maturity Model (KPI RMM™)

Responding to client requests that KPI survey the current state of the Business Rules Approach across industries in the United States, KPI undertook a study and formalized the findings in the KPI Rule Maturity Model (KPI RMM). The model includes a mapping to the business values, technology requisites, and governance issues of each level of maturity. It provides a roadmap for enterprises to adopt the Business Rules Approach, ensuring the highest return on investment while effectively managing risk. KPI has developed a range of techniques to leverage the power of the KPI RMM, and continues to validate the KPI RMM through wide ranging surveys of enterprises that have adopted or are about to adopt the Business Rules Approach.

KPI STEP™ License Program

In 2005 KPI announced a licensing program for the KPI STEP methodology. The objective was to provide a comprehensive and fully-supported environment for implementing the Business Rules Approach with a methodology that can be readily integrated into an existing project methodology. The license comprises the following sections (see the detailed illustration in Table 8):

- **How-to**: Step-by-step listings of project tasks and the appropriate input and output templates for each step, with training programs for rule harvesting, rule mining, and project planning, as well as comprehensive templates to be used with the "how-to" guides.

- **Software**: The KPI STEP Workbench as a comprehensive business rules repository and management system that fully supports KPI RMM Level 2, as well as software specifications and database schema to support up to KPI RMM Level 5, so that the licensee can build custom software should they so elect.

The KPI STEP License program is fully supported by KPI and its alliance partners of Consultants and Independent Service Providers. It includes a program of continuing improvements in the KPI STEP materials issued under the KPI STEP License Enhancement Program. The KPI STEP License can be purchased in the form of a Provisional License ("try-before-buy"), Project Level License, or Organization Level License (for organizations up to an enterprise level), and may be purchased through KPI alliance partners.

Table 8: A Subset of KPI STEP License Artifacts, Release 3.2.1

STEP-by-STEP How-To			KPI STEP Software	
General	Methods	Techniques	Software Specs	KPI STEP Workbench
Master matrix of tasks, templates, and samples	2-day *Rule Harvesting and Analysis* course	MS/Word templates	Software requirements correlated to RMM Level	Modeling capabilities, reporting, web-publishing, multi-user support
STOP paper on use cases and business rules				
	KPI Business Rules Applied	MS/Excel templates	Software requirements correlated to KPI STEP Workbench	KPI STEP and Business Rules Mining Reference Guide for the KPI STEP Workbench
Introduction to KPI RMM Part 1, 2	3-day *Business Rule Mining* course	PowerPoint samples	Logical Data Model to fully support KPI STEP	KPI STEP Workbench Install Guide
Beyond Business Rules Applied booklet, Issue 1	*Business Rule Mining* user guide	KPI STEP Workbench screen templates	Detailed Attribute Definitions	Pre-populated with KPI STEP Workshop Solutions

Printed in the United States
95629LV00002B/208-213/A